Resources for Teaching English: 11–14

Also available from Continuum

Resources for Teaching English: 14–16, David A. Hill
Resources for Teaching Creative Writing, Johnnie Young
Inspired English Teaching, Keith West
Teaching English using ICT, Chris Warren, Trevor Millum and Tom Rank
100+ Ideas for Teaching English, Angella Cooze
The English Teacher's Handbook, Helena Ceranic

Resources for Teaching English: 11–14

Helena Ceranic

continuum

A companion website to accompany this book is available online at:
http://education.ceranic.continuumbooks.com
Please visit the link and register with us to receive your password and access these
downloadable resources.
If you experience any problems accessing the resources, please contact Continuum at:
info@continuumbooks.com

Continuum International Publishing Group

The Tower Building	80 Maiden Lane
11 York Road	Suite 704
London	New York
SE1 7NX	NY 10038

www.continuumbooks.com

© Helena Ceranic 2011

Excerpt from *Down and Out in Paris and London*, copyright 1933 by George Orwell and
renewed 1961 by Sonia Pitt-Rivers, reprinted by permission of Houghton Mifflin Harcourt
Publishing Company.

British Library Cataloguing-in-Publication Data
A catalogue record for this book is available from the British Library.

ISBN: 978-1-4411-0211-9 (paperback)

Library of Congress Cataloging-in-Publication Data
Ceranic, Helena. Resources for teaching English : 11–14 / Helena Ceranic.
    p. cm. — (Resources for teaching series)
  Includes bibliographical references.
  ISBN 978-1-4411-0211-9 (pbk.) 1. Reading (Middle school) 2. Reading (Secondary)
3. Young adult literature—Study and teaching (Middle school) 4. Young adult literature—
Study and teaching (Secondary) I. Title. II. Series.
  LB1632.C4 2011   428.4071'2—dc22
  2010035663

Typeset by Pindar NZ, Auckland, New Zealand
Printed and bound in India

Contents

Section 1 Reading and writing non-fiction texts   1

Unit 1: Autobiographical writing   2

Unit 2: Travel writing   28

Unit 3: Writing for different audiences and purposes   54

Introduction

Planning good quality English lessons and resources can take a large amount of time and energy. This book has been designed to support the planning process by providing complete lesson plans with accompanying resources for 72 ready-to-teach hour-long English lessons, suitable for Key Stage 3 English (ages 11–14). Whether you are an experienced teacher or a classroom novice, these easy-to-use materials will help you to build up your repertoire of lesson plans. They could be used as one-off emergency lesson cover or integrated within existing or new schemes of work.

What the book contains

The book is divided into six units each containing 12 lessons that relate to English Curriculum National Strategy objectives for a particular year group, but many will be suitable for English lessons in other countries. The aims and objectives that link to the framework are listed on the companion website. The first three units cover reading and writing non-fiction texts:

1. Autobiographical writing (Year 7 – 11/12 years)
2. Travel writing (Year 8 – 12/13 years)
3. Writing for different audiences and purposes (Year 9 – 13/14 years)

The last three units address literary fiction:

4. Introducing Dickens (Year 7 – 11/12 years)
5. Exploring poetry (Year 8 – 12/13 years)
6. Engaging with Shakespeare (Year 9 – 13/14 years)

All three strands (reading, writing and speaking and listening) are addressed across the units of work. The four-part lesson plans refer to the English Curriculum National Strategy objectives for a particular year group and include suggestions for differentiation so that they can be used across Key Stage 3 (11–14 years) in setted and mixed-ability classrooms. The lessons stand alone but can also be taught as a unit of 12 lessons; in most instances the lessons follow on from previous ones so it would make sense to teach them in sequence.

How to use this book

The left-hand pages of the book (in the main) contain the lesson plan for the teacher. Each teacher sheet includes:
- an introduction to the lesson;
- an indication of any additional resources needed (e.g. dictionary);
- clear instructions for each stage of the lesson, with approximate timeframes;
- homework ideas;
- suggestions for extension or support.

The right-hand pages (in the main) contain accompanying resources in the form of photocopiable task sheets for students. These are also available online so that you can print them if you prefer. (Please note that the online task sheets for lessons 1:10, 2:1, 2:12 and 3:7 do not contain the extract or cover images and therefore it would be best to photocopy these from the book.) For some lessons there is more than one resource page to allow for additional text extracts or kinaesthetic materials.

Some lessons require access to dictionaries or computers, and where these apply you will clearly see an icon on the lesson plan, but in most cases only the accompanying task sheet is necessary, keeping the lessons simple and straightforward to prepare and deliver. Suggested homework tasks are also provided for each lesson; they have been designed to extend students' learning and should be quick and easy to explain before or after the plenary activity.

Some of the lessons lend themselves to additional notes or support materials, and where you see the relevant icon these 'cheat sheets' can be accessed online. At the same site you will also find a list of web links that feature in the lesson plans.

Key

 Dictionary required

 Access to computer required

 Video camera required

 Cheat sheet available online

Section 1 Reading and writing non-fiction texts

Introducing autobiographical and biographical writing

Introduction

This lesson is an introduction to autobiographical writing. It gives students the opportunity to explore prefixes in order to understand the root meaning of 'biography' and 'autobiography'. Students look at book covers in an attempt to identify the difference between the two forms of text. They then sort extracts according to their use of pronouns and evaluate their effectiveness at engaging the reader.

Aims and objectives

- Increase knowledge of word families, roots, derivations, morphology and regular spelling patterns.
- Make a personal response to a text and provide some textual reference in support.

Starter (10 minutes)

Allocate prefixes to groups of students (sub, auto, inter, etc.). Explain that a prefix is part of a word that is at the beginning and changes the meaning. Ask each group to generate a list of words that start with their allocated prefix. They look at the meaning of the words that they have listed and try to devise a definition for the prefix, using dictionaries to check definitions.

Main phase (40 minutes)

- Feed back prefix definitions and examples to the class. Focus on the prefixes 'auto' and 'bio' and use these as the basis for writing a definition of autobiography and biography. Students answer the following questions:
    - *What is the difference between an autobiography and a biography?* (autobiographies are written by the subject; biographies are written by another author about the subject)
    - *Why do people enjoy reading these texts?* (curiosity/admiration . . .)
    - *Which one would you prefer to read and why?*
- Introduce the learning objectives and lesson outcomes: to analyse and evaluate autobiographical and biographical book jackets and extracts.
- Display/distribute the David Beckham book jacket to groups of students. Ask students to identify whether they think the cover is from a biography or an autobiography, using clues from the text and images. Discuss ideas and justify with evidence and reference to the first person pronoun.
- Look at the extracts from various autobiographical and biographical texts on the following task sheet and sort them into two text types based on the use of the first or third person.

Plenary (10 minutes)

Ask the students to select one extract that they would like to read more of. They should explain their choice in a short paragraph and be ready to share this with the rest of the class.

Homework ideas

Ask students to visit a bookshop or library and read the book jackets of three other autobiographies/biographies. They need to make notes about the texts to feed back to the class in the next lesson.

Make it easier!

Complete the text-sort activity as a whole class, discussing rationale for choices.

Make it harder!

Students create their own sentences about their lives and then change them into the third person.

1:1 Introducing autobiographical and biographical writing – prefix cards

auto	poly
trans	aero
inter	dis
sub	co
tele	bio
aud	mono

David Beckham: My side by David Beckham and Tom Watt, is reproduced with the permission of HarperCollins Publishers Ltd © 2003.

1:1 Introducing autobiographical and biographical writing – extracts from autobiographies and biographies

I can't bear ice in my drinks – it always makes me think of the iceberg, you see.	Like any single young lady back then, she went to dances and flirted with eligible young men.
Judy married John Blume on August 12, 1959.	I was two-and-three-quarters when I started school and it was a traumatic time.
Suddenly, Beckham jerked his right foot up and his heel struck Simeone.	It was mother who first saw that there was something wrong with me. I was about four months old at the time.
When I was held hostage I tried to remember my childhood, but I could never get beyond the age of eight or nine.	They created the kingdom of Gondal and wrote all kinds of epic stories and poems set in that realm.
Although he worked hard and was well paid enough, his family lived constantly on the brink of poverty.	From then on, all through the winter, I became Wilberforce's favourite bog-seat warmer.

Comparing autobiographies and biographies

Introduction

This lesson invites students to identify the similarities and differences between autobiographical and biographical texts. In comparing accounts, students discuss the benefits and limitations of each type of text. They also examine the use of fact and opinion before considering the relative reliability and entertainment factor of both forms of writing.

Aims and objectives

* Make informed personal choices of texts and express their preferences.
* Describe and find examples of how language is used in different contexts.

Starter (10 minutes)

Hand out the accompanying task sheet. Students discuss the six statements and complete the grid according to whether they consider the text features to belong to autobiographical writing or biographical writing.

Main phase (40 minutes)

* Discuss decisions made in the starter activity and consider any statements that could be features of both types of text. Students consider the following questions in pairs; they will return to these at the end of the lesson.
  — *Which type of text is most reliable – autobiography or biography? Why?*
  — *Which type of text is more interesting to read – autobiography or biography? Why?*
* Introduce the learning objectives and lesson outcomes: to compare two texts to ascertain the similarities and differences between an exemplar autobiography and biography.
* Introduce George Orwell and explain who he was:

www.notablebiographies.com/Ni-Pe/Orwell-George

* Read the extract on the task sheet from Orwell's novel *Down and Out in Paris and London*. Discuss the impression we get of Orwell and his situation, and the writing style used.
* Read the next extract, taken from the Wikipedia entry about George Orwell and compare the content and style of the two texts. Ask students to write a paragraph comparing them. Students need to consider which one seems most reliable/trustworthy/interesting and why.

Plenary (10 minutes)

Return to the questions posed at the start of the lesson. Students should answer these in their books, reflecting on what they noticed in the George Orwell extracts.

Homework ideas

Ask students to use the internet to research George Orwell and create a fact sheet about him.

Make it easier!

Provide students with the following starter sentences to support their comparative paragraph:

Orwell's autobiography has a more entertaining writing style, for example . . .

The Wikipedia entry makes the reader realise that . . .

Make it harder!

Identify facts and opinions within the two extracts and consider the balance used.

1:2 Comparing autobiographies and biographies

Draw the following grid in your book and then add the text features below to each column, after discussion.

Autobiographical writing	Biographical writing

1. The author gives an objective account of events.
2. The author can describe how he/she felt at the time of an event.
3. The author can leave out events that are embarrassing or personal.
4. The author covers all of the events in the life story.
5. The author is detached from what he/she is writing about.
6. The author can be biased or exaggerate certain events.

> My money oozed away – to eight francs, to four francs, to one franc, to twenty-five centimes; and twenty-five centimes is useless, for it will buy nothing except a newspaper. We went several days on dry bread, and then I was two and a half days with nothing to eat whatever. This was an ugly experience. There are people who do fasting cures of three weeks or more, and they say that fasting is quite pleasant after the fourth day; I do not know, never having gone beyond the third day. Probably it seems different when one is doing it voluntarily and is not underfed at the start.

Taken from *Down and Out in Paris and London* by George Orwell. (Copyright © George Orwell, 1933) Reprinted by permission of Bill Hamilton as the Literary Executor of the Estate of the Late Sonia Brownell Orwell and Secker & Warburg Ltd.

> In the spring of 1928, he moved to Paris, where the comparatively low cost of living and bohemian lifestyle offered an attraction for many aspiring writers. His Aunt Nellie Limouzin also lived there and gave him social and, if necessary, financial support. He worked on novels, but only *Burmese Days* survives from that activity. More successful as a journalist, he published articles in *Monde* (not to be confused with *Le Monde*), *G. K.'s Weekly* and *Le Progres Civique* (founded by the left-wing coalition Le Cartel des Gauches).
>
> He fell seriously ill in March 1929 and shortly afterwards had all his money stolen from the lodging house. Whether through necessity or simply to collect material, he undertook menial jobs like dishwashing in a fashionable hotel on the rue de Rivoli providing experiences to be used in *Down and Out in Paris and London*.

Taken from http://en.wikipedia.org/wiki/George_Orwell

Questioning skills and mini-biographies

Introduction

In this lesson, students study different questioning styles, including closed and open questions, in preparation for peer interviews. Students are given the opportunity to write mini-biographies to practise the skill of writing an account in the third person. Evaluation of students' writing focuses on the quality of the information included.

Aims and objectives

- Recognize different conventions and forms in speech.
- Develop their own viewpoint, drawing on evidence, opinions and the particular purpose of the task.

Starter (15 minutes)

Discuss different questioning styles and complete the definitions on the task sheet. Students interview each other in pairs using the questions on the task sheet. They should then decide what kinds of questions they have used and circle the corresponding initial in the boxes provided, i.e. O = open, C = closed R = rhetorical, L = leading.

Main phase (35 minutes)

- Evaluate the quality of the different types of questions using the following prompts:
  — *Which questions provided brief, factual answers?* (closed)
  — *Which questions allowed the respondent to give detailed, opinionated answers?* (open)
  — *Which questions were difficult to answer? Why?* (rhetorical and leading – assumed a given answer)
- Introduce the learning objectives and lesson outcomes: students interview each other and create mini-biographies.
- Students create ten questions of their own to ask their partner about their childhood. They should try to include a range of open questions to provide scope for personal, detailed responses.
- Students take it in turns to interview each other using their questions and make notes in their books. They then write up their findings into a potted biography.

Plenary (10 minutes)

Ask students to swap their biographies with another pair in the class. They need to read and evaluate the quality and breadth of information included. Share findings and opinions with the rest of the class.

Homework ideas

Ask students to interview an elderly member of their family to find out about their childhood. Students must write a paragraph on how their relative's experiences differ from their own.

Make it easier!

Supply students with a range of questions to start off their interviews:
- What is your earliest memory?
- What was your favourite childhood toy?
- What can you remember about your first friends?

Make it harder!

Ask students to review sentence openings used in the mini-biographies and try to vary the phrasing used to avoid all sentences starting with names or pronouns.

1:3 Questioning skills and mini-biographies

1. Write in the definitions for the different styles of questions below.

   Closed questions . . . .

   Open questions . . . .

   Rhetorical questions . . . .

   Leading questions . . . .

   - How old are you?

     O C R L

   - What are your opinions on chocolate?

     O C R L

   - How do you get to school?

     O C R L

   - What do you think about Harry Potter?

     O C R L

   - You don't like watching the news do you?

     O C R L

   - What is the point of this interview anyway?

     O C R L

2. Write down ten questions to ask your partner about their childhood for your mini-biography interview.

   1. . . . .

   2. . . . .

   3. . . . .

   4. . . . .

   5. . . . .

   6. . . . .

   7. . . . .

   8. . . . .

   9. . . . .

   10. . . . .

Recounting memories

Introduction

This lesson introduces students to the term 'literary non-fiction' and asks them to identify the literary techniques used in a piece of autobiographical description. Students then write their own account of a memorable event, using some of the literary features to bring their memory to life.

Aims and objectives

- Identify and describe the effect of writers' use of specific literary, rhetorical and grammatical features.
- Develop in their own writing some of the key linguistic and literary techniques used by writers, and deploy them for deliberate effect on the reader.

Starter (5 minutes)

Ask students to complete the following sentence: *My parents embarrass me when they . . .* Share sentence endings and discuss experiences.

Main phase (50 minutes)

- Introduce the piece of autobiographical description on the task sheet and explain that it is an example of literary non-fiction. Explore this term and consider:
  — *the features of literature texts* (narrative, character description, imagery)
  — *the features of non-fiction texts* (facts, real-life events)
  — *why authors might use literary features in their non-fiction texts* (entertainment, interest).
- Create a definition for this term and ask students to make notes in their books.
- Introduce the learning objectives and lesson outcomes: to analyse a piece of literary non-fiction and use similar techniques to write about a vivid memory.
- Read the autobiographical extract and highlight evidence of linguistic features such as sensory description and rhetorical questions that are used to bring the scene to life. Discuss the text and ask students to select a couple of quotes to analyse in their books.
- Invite students to reflect on a vivid memory from their own childhood and answer the questions on the task sheet. Students use their responses to write a description of their memory, using a range of linguistic techniques.

Plenary (5 minutes)

Each student selects an effective sentence from their description to read aloud to the rest of the class. Share extracts in the form of a Mexican wave of contributions across the room.

Homework ideas

Ask students to watch the trailer for the film *And When Did You last See Your Father?*, based on a book by Blake Morrison in which he reflects on his childhood (www.imdb.com/video/screenplay/vi269549593), and write a mini-review including their first impressions of the film.

Make it easier!

Model annotation of the text by completing it with the class (see cheat sheet).

Make it harder!

Ask students to focus on sentence length and range of vocabulary used in the extract and ensure that their own description includes a variety of sentence types and sophisticated words.

1:4 Recounting memories

I moved primary schools aged nine. We relocated to a new town so I was uprooted like a little sapling; having enjoyed the environment and nourishment of a pool of friends in a school that I loved, I had to adjust to a whole new climate. My parents were not going to make this traumatic change easy for me . . .

It was a hot and sunny July day and I was standing at the gates of my new school. My mum had decided that it would be a good idea for us to attend my new school's summer fête before starting there in September. It should have been a fun day; a chance for me to familiarise myself with new surroundings and meet new friends. However, my parents decided to make it one of the most embarrassing days of my little life.

As we entered the school field we were met by a cacophany of different sounds, sights and smells: the chatter of enthusiastic children; the scent of barbequed meats wafting towards us; an array of exciting games and activities to take part in. The children looked like a throng of best friends; a community of little ants happily playing together. I didn't want to stand out as an outsider, I wanted to blend into the background. So why did Dad decide to become the centre of attention?

Within seconds, he had spotted the huge bouncy castle, shaped like a giant octopus, and made a beeline for it. He clambered onto the purple plastic and leapt crazily up and down, sending small children around him flying off in all directions. Concerned parents ran to their children's rescue, shooting disapproving glares at Dad who clearly didn't realise that the bouncy castle was there for children to enjoy, not for the amusement of middle-aged men. He carried on bouncing maniacally, oblivious of the collateral damage he was causing. He started to wave crazily at me, telling me to come and join him. I tried to avoid eye contact and pretend that I didn't know him. Mum then grabbed my hand and dragged me begrudgingly across the field to join Dad. I could hear the river of whispers from children and parents alike: 'Who's that girl?'; 'Is she with that idiot?' My faced flushed red like an overripe tomato in sheer embarrassment. Still, I wasn't prepared for what was about to ensue . . .

I neared the edge of the bouncy castle just as my Dad decided to show off with a huge star jump. An enormous ripping sound caught the attention of everyone on the field who turned round to witness Dad's shorts splitting in two to reveal his garish Simpsons Y fronts. That image is still imprinted on my brain. The shame of it!

From that moment on I was referred to as 'Pant Girl' at my new school. Thanks Dad, thanks a lot.

Think of a significant memory from your childhood. Answer the following questions about the event to help to bring it to life:

1. How old were you?
....
2. Who was there and what happened?
....
3. What could you hear/see/smell?
....
4. How did you feel?
....

Starting secondary school

Introduction

This lesson asks students to reflect on their first day at secondary school. The activities require them to discuss their memories and feelings in pairs and use their listening skills to make notes for each other. After selecting specific vocabulary and experiences to express their memories, the final outcome is to produce a poem based on their personal experiences.

Aims and objectives

- Identify, sift and summarize the most important points or key ideas from a talk or discussion.
- Develop character and voice in their own fiction writing.

Starter (10 minutes)

Circulate the task sheet. Ask students to select the faces that best represent their feelings at different stages of their first day at secondary school and explain their choices to their partner. Swap over and share with the class.

Main phase (45 minutes)

- Introduce the learning objectives and lesson outcomes: to produce a poem that reflects their memories of their first day at secondary school.
- Ask students to generate adjectives to describe their feelings on their first day. Model how to place the words on a line depending on their level of positivity/negativity. Ask students to complete this activity on their task sheets using their own adjectives.
- In pairs, ask students to recount their experiences of their first day at secondary school, using the prompt questions on the task sheet. The listening partner needs to make notes; summarising the key events and feelings that have been described to them. Students swap over after five minutes.
- Students hand their notes to each other and then start to create their own poems based on their experiences. They should refer to the adjectives they have generated as well.

Plenary (5 minutes)

Each student selects an effective sentence from their description to read aloud to the rest of the class. Share extracts in the form of a Mexican wave of contributions across the room.

Homework ideas

Ask students to create an illustrated version of their poem for display.

Make it easier!

Provide students with examples of 'first day at school' poems to use as a model, such as Roger McGough's:

www.poemhunter.com/poem/first-day-at-school/

Make it harder!

Ask students to write their poem based on their partner's experiences of their first day at school rather than their own.

1:5 Starting secondary school

1. Think back to your first day at secondary school. Which of the expressions below show how you felt:

   - before you got to school
   - halfway through the day
   - at the end of the day?

   Discuss and share your memories with your partner.

2. Now select adjectives to describe your feelings on your first day at secondary school. Plot them on the line below depending on whether the word describes a positive (right), negative (left), or neutral (middle) feeling.

   Negative   **Positive**

   –

3. Cast your mind back to that day and think of all of the things that you can recall about it. For example:

   - How did you get to school?
   - What lessons did you have?
   - What did you do at break and lunchtime?
   - What was your favourite part of the day?
   - What was your least favourite part?
   - Did you get lost?

   Share your memories and feelings with your partner and try to explain them. Ask your partner to make notes for you while you are speaking.

4. Now use all your notes and memories to create a poem about your first day at secondary school. You can choose to use rhyme and rhythm if you wish.

Letter to primary school

Introduction

In this lesson, students get the opportunity to write a letter to their primary school teacher, informing them of how they are getting on at secondary school. The first part of the lesson prompts students to generate ideas and create a plan; the second part focuses on the written outcome and making sure that the language used is appropriate for audience and purpose.

Aims and objectives

- Develop different ways of generating, organizing and shaping ideas, using a range of planning formats or methods.
- Understand and use degrees of formality in a range of texts according to context, purpose and audience.

Starter (10 minutes)

Get students to chart the differences between primary and secondary school on the Venn diagram provided on the task sheet. You may need to explain the principles of this planning tool and model it for the students.

Discuss students' ideas and reflect on how they have changed since settling in to secondary school.

Main phase (45 minutes)

- Introduce the learning objectives and lesson outcomes: to produce a letter that will be sent to their primary school letting their old teachers know how they are getting on. Ask students to remember their target audience and consider what would and wouldn't be appropriate to include in the letter.
- Ask students to compile a spider diagram, like the one on the task sheet, with ideas to include in their letter. They may wish to consider school routines, favourite subjects, new hobbies and friends, for example.
- Review ideas and focus on the need to structure and order ideas into paragraphs. Ask students to group together similar topics and create a paragraph structure before starting to draft their letters.

Plenary (5 minutes)

Swap letter drafts and ask students to check that the style of writing is suitably formal and polite for the given target audience.

Homework ideas

Ask students to complete a final draft of their letter and send it to their primary school.

Make it easier!

Revise the standard layout for a formal letter and how to address an envelope properly:

www.business-letter.org/wp-content/uploads/2009/09/business-letter-template.gif/
www.weddingstamps.co.uk/assets/new_envelope_rev1.jpg/

Make it harder!

Get students to self-edit the drafts of their letters to check for suitability and accuracy.

1:6 Letter to primary school

1. Chart the differences between primary and secondary school in the Venn diagram below – place any similarities in the section in the middle.

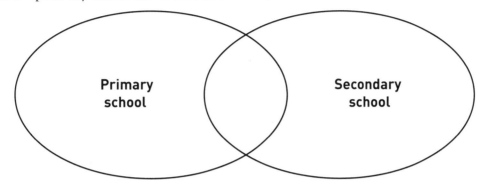

2. Create a spider diagram including all of your ideas for your letter. What information do you want to tell your primary teacher? What significant things have happened since you started secondary school? (Do this on a separate piece of paper, using the diagram below as a guide.)

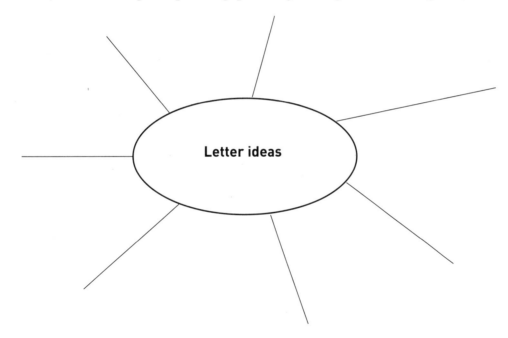

3. Now review all your ideas and choose which ones you will include in your letter and in what order. Try to group together ideas that relate to the same topic, e.g. information about subjects, teachers and homework could all go into a paragraph about lessons. Plan your paragraph content below:

1. ....

2. ....

3. ....

4. ....

My favourite celebrity

Introduction
In this lesson, students consider influential celebrities whom they admire. They source material about their chosen celebrity and prepare for an individual presentation to the rest of the class. Students have to collate relevant information and any other appropriate resources, such as images, film or music clips, to add to their presentations.

Aims and objectives
- Extract the main points and relevant information from a text or source using a range of strategies such as skimming and scanning.
- Use some verbal and non-verbal techniques to make talk interesting for listeners.

Starter (10 minutes)
Introduce the term 'celebrity' and try to define its meaning and the breadth of different types of people that it covers. Ask students to put the celebrities on the task sheet in rank order according to how influential they are and how much they admire them; feed back ideas.

Main phase (40 minutes)
- Introduce the learning objectives and lesson outcomes: to prepare an individual presentation to perform in front of the class on the topic of 'my favourite celebrity'. Explain to the students the need to research relevant information and material to keep their audience interested and engaged.
- Get students to log on to the internet. Discuss searching and note-making strategies such as skimming and scanning. Encourage students to note down key information rather than copying and pasting huge chunks of text.
- Ask students to organise the information they have sourced into a presentation. Compile *PowerPoint* presentations with an emphasis on being selective about the text and images they choose to have on the slides.

Plenary (10 minutes)
Generate a list of the dos and don'ts of effective presentations. Discuss the types of verbal and non-verbal techniques students could use to make their delivery more lively and engaging.

Homework ideas
Ask students to create a collage for display with images associated with their favourite celebrity.

Make it easier!
Provide students with a *PowerPoint* template to add their information to so that they can focus on the presentation's content.

Make it harder!
Introduce the term 'Death by *PowerPoint*' (a term that refers to the state of boredom and fatigue caused by poor presentations that include information overload, poor design and/or ineffectual delivery techniques) and develop a list of stylistic rules for students to follow, such as consistent colour schemes, not merely reading the text from the slides, and having an equal balance of text and images. If possible, observe examples of presentations for students to evaluate before starting to deliver their own. For more information on 'Death by *PowerPoint*' visit:

www.thinkoutsidetheslide.com/articles/avoid_death_by_ppt.htm/

1:7 My favourite celebrity

1. What is the definition of a celebrity?

   Celebrity (noun): . . . .

2. Consider the following celebrities and rank them in order of how much you admire them. Discuss what qualities and skills they have and whether these influence you.

   Jenson Button

   Madonna

   Barrack Obama

   Paula Radcliffe

   Brad Pitt

3. Who is your favourite celebrity and why?

   . . . .
   . . . .
   . . . .
   . . . .
   . . . .

4. Use the internet to research the celebrity of your choice. Make notes in the box below.

Dreams and ambitions for the future

Introduction

In this lesson, students share their dreams and ambitions for the future. Once they have revised the features of writing to explain, including the use of connectives, students outline their dreams and ambitions for the future in an informative and detailed way. Peer discussion prompts students to include additional justification.

Aims and objectives

- Draw on the conventions of written forms to plan writing and develop ideas to fit a specific task.
- Make ideas and purpose clear by appropriate use of paragraphs and by choosing from a range of linking words and phrases.

Starter (10 minutes)

Ask students to discuss the difference between dreams and ambitions. Get them to draw symbols that represent their own dreams and ambitions for the future in the dream cloud on the task sheet (for example pound signs to denote wealth), and discuss.

Main phase (40 minutes)

- Introduce the learning objectives and lesson outcomes: to write a detailed piece of explanation outlining their own dreams and ambitions for the future. Discuss the features of this style of writing and the importance of explaining reasons and motivations.
- Get students to generate a list of connective phrases in the box on the task sheet that will enable them to elaborate on their explanation, for example because, therefore, in addition.
- Ask students to complete the boxes at the bottom of the task sheet with details and reasons that will help them to explain their dreams and ambitions. Model the process with an example on the board, such as:
  — Dream: to be a midwife.
  — Reasons: job satisfaction; helping others; being a part of patients' happiest moments.

Plenary (10 minutes)

Ask students to challenge each other by talking through their notes and asking each other the questions 'how?' and 'why?' to encourage them to include additional reasons and details.

Homework ideas

Ask students to complete their explanations of their dreams and ambitions for the future.

Make it easier!

Write an exemplary paragraph together as a class to model the writing style.

Make it harder!

Write up the dreams and ambitions into paragraphs using connectives and notes.

1:8 Dreams and ambitions for the future

1. Draw images in the cloud below to represent your dreams and ambitions for the future.

2. Create a bank of connectives in the box below – these will help you to link your ideas and explain your reasons.

3. Use the boxes below to select your important dreams/ambitions and add reasons and details in the space on the right.

Dream/ambition		Details/reasons for this choice
	→	
	→	
	→	
	→	

Time capsule tasks

Introduction

In this lesson, students explore the purpose of a time capsule and devise and justify their own items to be included in one. The second part of the lesson involves them writing the speech for a podcast to be included in the time capsule. Students need to demonstrate an ability to speak with clarity and purpose.

Aims and objectives

- Make clear and relevant contributions to group discussion, promoting, opposing, exploring and questioning as appropriate.
- Tailor the structure and vocabulary of talk to clarify ideas and guide the listener.

Starter (10 minutes)

Introduce the term 'time capsule' (http://uk.encarta.msn.com/dictionary_1861750736/time_capsule.html?qpvt=what+is+a+time+capsule). Ask students to discuss what they know about these objects – what are they used for? Explore this together as a class and ask students to come up with a list of five things that they would include in their own time capsule, with reasons (write notes on the task sheet).

Main phase (40 minutes)

- Introduce the learning objectives and lesson outcomes: to decide on the contents of a time capsule, as a group, that will be opened in 50 years' time, and produce the script for a podcast that will be included. Organise groups and answer any questions about the task.
- In groups, students discuss individual ideas for the time capsule contents and agree on the best five to be included in the group's capsule. Students will need to practise and develop their discussion skills to agree on an outcome in a limited amount of time (5 minutes).
- Once the items have been agreed on, students need to share out responsibility for explaining the individual items: their purpose, function and importance. They will then write up the speech to accompany their designated item, making sure that the language used is suitably clear and easy to follow.

Plenary (10 minutes)

Share speeches among the groups and critically evaluate their content and style. Students need to check that the explanation is detailed enough for future listeners to understand.

Homework ideas

Ask students to collate pictures of items that they would include in their time capsule, adding accompanying captions for display.

Make it easier!

Provide students with a list of objects for consideration to include in their time capsule, such as photographs, a PlayStation game, coins, etc.

Make it harder!

Record the speeches using electronic devices such as a laptop microphone, dictaphone or mobile phone recorder to enable students to practise speaking for their specified audience.

1:9 Time capsule tasks

1. What is a time capsule? (Answer this question with a definition and examples.)

   . . . .

   . . . .

2. Generate a list of five items that you would choose to include in a time capsule, with reasons.

   1. . . . .

   2. . . . .

   3. . . . .

   4. . . . .

   5. . . . .

3. Once you have discussed ideas within a group and agreed on five items between you, draw (or write) these in the capsule below.

4. Write notes for your section of the podcast speech below. The following prompts may help:

   - What purpose does this object/item serve?

   - Why have you chosen to include it?

   - Why is it a precious or significant object?

   - What does it reveal about the way of life at this particular period of time?

Anne Frank's diary

Introduction

In this lesson, students develop their understanding of Anne Frank through sharing prior knowledge and learning more about her experiences as described in her diary. After discussing hardships suffered by Jews during the Second World War, students get the chance to demonstrate their empathetic writing skills.

Aims and objectives

- Use inference and deduction to recognize implicit meanings at sentence and text level.
- Understand the different ways texts can reflect the social, cultural and historical contexts in which they were written.

Starter (10 minutes)

Ask students to share their knowledge of Anne Frank, her life and her diary and record this information around the picture of the diary cover on the task sheet. They should look at the book jacket image for further clues. Explain that Anne was a Jewish girl whose family hid in an attic above her father's factory during the Second World War to escape from the Nazis. She kept a secret diary from the age of 13, recording her experiences. The diary was published after her death in a concentration camp, and has become extremely popular worldwide.

Main phase (45 minutes)

- Introduce the learning objectives and explain that students will have the chance to extend their knowledge of Anne Frank by exploring her experiences in the diary.
- Explain that the task sheet contains several facts about how Jewish people were treated during the Second World War, as described in Anne Frank's diary. Ask students to discuss each fact one by one in groups and consider how the rules would have made Jewish people feel, making notes on their sheets.
- Then ask students to use their notes to write a paragraph in the voice of a Jewish child during the Second World War, explaining how they feel about their treatment.

Plenary (5 minutes)

Ask students to discuss why the diary of a young Jewish girl written during this period has become such a popular text translated into so many languages. Consider how and why the diary might successfully reflect its social and historical context.

Homework ideas

Ask students to research these websites dedicated to Anne Frank and write a paragraph reviewing them for the quality of their information and design:

> www.annefrank.org
> www.annefrank.com

Make it easier!

Use extracts from video versions of Anne Frank's diary to bring the diary's events to life. There are several different versions available on YouTube.

Make it harder!

Provide students with extracts from *The Diary of a Young Girl* to use during the main part of the lesson.

Note: The online task sheet does not contain the cover image of *The Diary of a Young Girl*.

1:10 Anne Frank's diary

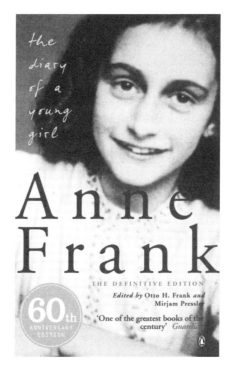

Cover image of *The Diary of A Young Girl: The Definitive Edition* by Anne Frank, edited by Otto H. Frank and Mirjam Pressler, translated by Susan Massotty (Viking 1997), copyright © The Anne Frank-Fonds, Basle, Switzerland, 1991, English translation copyright. Doubleday, a division of Doubleday Dell Publishing Group Inc, 1995.

- Jewish people could only go to the shops between 3 and 5 o'clock in the afternoon.

- Jewish people were not allowed to use any kind of transport; they had to hand in their bicycles and couldn't ride on the tram or in their own cars.

- Jews had to pin a yellow star on their clothing to show everyone that they were Jewish.

- Jews could only get their hair cut at Jewish salons.

- A night-time curfew was enforced upon Jewish people; they were not allowed out between 8 p.m. and 6 a.m.

- Jewish people were not allowed to use any kind of leisure facility and could not do any form of exercise in public.

The Princess Diaries

Introduction

This lesson introduces students to the fictional character, Mia Thermopolis, the heroine of Meg Cabot's *The Princess Diaries*. First, students explore the Americanisms and consider how colloquial language can create a sense of character. Once students have watched extracts from the film, they write their own diary entry in the style of Mia.

Aims and objectives

- Identify some of the ways in which spoken English varies in different regions and settings.
- Develop in their own writing some of the key linguistic and literary techniques used by writers, and deploy them for deliberate effect on the reader.

Starter (15 minutes)

Get students to write a diary extract based on what they did yesterday. Ask students whether their diaries could be published, and why. Discuss the idea that published diaries need to include interesting events and have an engaging writing style.

Main phase (35 minutes)

- Introduce the learning objectives and task sheet. Read the list of words and ask students to identify their origin and their English equivalents. Introduce the term 'Americanisms' and ask students to think of two more examples and add them to their task sheet with the Standard English translations.
- Introduce *The Princess Diaries* and explain that Meg Cabot, the author, writes using American English and a range of colloquialisms (informal language) to help to bring the central character to life.
- Play students the film trailer for *The Princess Diaries* (www.imdb.com/title/tt0247638) and ask them to make notes about what happens to Mia on their task sheet.
- Ask students now to transform the diary entries and make them more exciting by adding events that they witnessed happening to Mia in the trailer.

Plenary (10 minutes)

Ask students to swap their diaries within groups of four and select the most entertaining use of language. Share these examples and award a class winner.

Homework ideas

Ask students to create an extract from Mia's diary, including a range of entries and focusing on creative presentation to make it look like the real article.

Make it easier!

Watch the additional clips from the film, available on YouTube to help students get a better impression of Mia's character.

Make it harder!

Ask students to include a range of Americanisms and colloquialisms in their diary extracts to make them sound more authentic.

1:11 The Princess Diaries

1. Look at the list of vocabulary below. What do you notice about all of these words? Now write down the Standard English equivalents next to them. If you don't know the meaning of all of the words, discuss with others.

mom

recess

fries

mall

sneakers

vacation

candy

freshman

2. *The Princess Diaries* is a book based on the diary of a fictional character, Mia Thermopolis, who is an average teenage school girl until she finds out that she is a member of the Genovian royal family and about to become princess. Watch the trailer for the film based on the book and make notes in the box below about what you see happening to Mia.

3. Now write a diary entry as Mia in the space below, using your notes. Try to use an entertaining style and include American vocabulary.

Dear Diary

....

....

....

....

....

....

....

....

....

Identity task

Introduction

In this lesson, students reflect on their own identity through some autobiographical activities. First of all they design a crest that represents their personality. They then create a collage using various images that have links to the things that are important to them. Students use these identity maps to support individual presentations about themselves.

Aims and objectives

- Use some verbal and non-verbal techniques to make talk interesting for listeners.
- Develop different ways of generating, organizing and shaping ideas, using a range of planning formats or methods.

Starter (10 minutes)

Introduce the concept of crests and coats of arms and the way in which they represent a person or family. Ask students to design their own crest on the task sheet. They should choose symbols and objects that show something about their tastes or personality.

Main phase (40 minutes)

- Share and discuss students' crests and ask individuals to explain what they have included and why.
- Explain that the main activity is an extension of the starter: students will create an identity map – a collage that represents their personality. They can use computers or magazines to source images and text for their collages.
- Tell students that they will be asked to present their identity maps and they have 5 minutes to prepare, without notes, using their collage as a prop and prompt.

Plenary (10 minutes)

Select a few students to present their collages; remaining students should get involved by asking pertinent questions about items that have not been explained by the presenters.

Homework ideas

Ask students to write an accompanying commentary for their identity maps that can be displayed alongside them.

Make it easier!

Provide students with a range of pre-cut images to select from instead of having to source them themselves.

Make it harder!

Distribute speaking and listening level criteria to students and ask them to peer-assess the presentations.

1:12 Identity task

1. Crests are a form of identification, originally worn by soldiers on their helmets. They include symbols, for example a lion to denote strength. In the template below, design your own crest to represent you. Draw in objects that have significance for you.

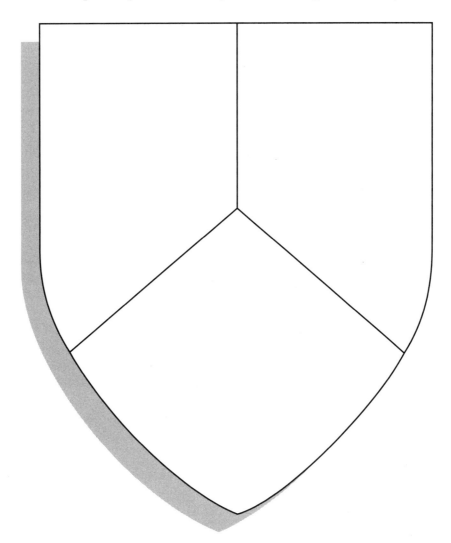

2. On a separate piece of paper you are now going to create an identity map – a collage of images and text that represents your personality and interests. Using the internet or magazines, source the content to display on your identity map.

Travel writing texts and preferences

Introduction

In this lesson, students are introduced to travel writing texts and consider the different audiences, purposes and styles within this genre. Students discuss their own holiday preferences by sorting through a range of holiday options. They then design their own dream holiday, building on their discussions and experiences.

Aims and objectives

- Make a sustained contribution to group discussion, and illustrate and explain their ideas.
- Explore, problem-solve, connect and shape ideas, and identify the most appropriate approach to planning their writing.

Starter (10 minutes)

Ask students to look at the two book covers on the first task sheet and discuss who they think the books are aimed at and what they expect them to contain. Explain that the titles below the images also belong to travel writing texts and ask students to consider the different impressions they get of the books from the language used.

Main phase (45 minutes)

- Introduce learning objectives and observations from the starter activity. Explain that this lesson is a chance for students to reflect on their own holiday experiences before reading and creating pieces of travel writing.
- In groups, ask students to discuss the holiday options on the second task sheet and sort them from best to worst. This will involve students justifying their opinions and supporting their views. Students then write down their choices individually.
- Students then design their own dream holiday by jotting ideas in the dream clouds on the next task sheet and filling in the holiday preferences grid.

Plenary (5 minutes)

Ask students to consider whether any of the travel writing texts from the starter are of interest to them, based on their own holiday preferences and interests. Discuss as a class.

Homework ideas

Ask students to create a poster for their dream holiday, including a slogan and a range of associated images.

Make it easier!

Show students an example of a holiday poster to support their homework task or help to stimulate discussion of dream holiday preferences.

www.allposters.com/-sp/Hawaii-Land-of-Surf-and-Sunshine-Posters_i382285_.htm/

Make it harder!

Ask students to decide which one of the travel writing titles (in the starter activity) is the most appealing to them and explain their reasoning.

Note: The first online task sheet for this lesson does not contain the cover images of *The Rough Guide to First-Time Around the World* and *The Happy Campers*.

 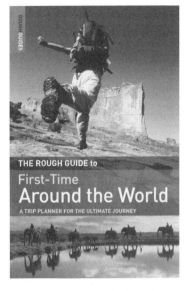

The Happy Campers by Tess Carr and Kat Heyes (2007) is reproduced with the permission of Bloomsbury Publishing PLC.

The Rough Guide to First-Time Around the World edited by Doug Lansky (Rough Guides 2003, 2006), copyright © Rough Guides 2003, is reproduced with the permission of The Penguin Group.

Consider the **audience**, **purpose** and **style** of these travel writing titles. Consider who you think would be interested in each of the texts and why, according to the language used.

A The *Happy Campers: Camping-fun-life-fire-food-love* by Tess Carr and Kat Heyes . . . .
. . . .

B *The Rough Guide to First-Time Around The World: A trip planner for the ultimate journey* . . . .
. . . .

C *Notes from a Small Island* by Bill Bryson . . . .
. . . .

D *Notes From The Hard Shoulder* by James May . . . .
. . . .

E *Unforgettable Places to See Before You Die* by Steve Davey . . . .
. . . .

2:1 Travel writing texts and preferences – holiday preferences

What would be your preferred holiday and why? Discuss the options below within your groups and then justify your choice below.

- Skiing with friends in the Alps
- All inclusive beach holiday with boyfriend/girlfriend in the Caribbean
- Teenage adventure break in the Amazon
- Safari with tour group in South Africa
- Road trip with strangers across North America
- Swimming with dolphins in Australia
- City break in Rome with parents

My choice of holiday would be . . . .

My reasons for this are . . . .

. . . .

. . . .

. . . .

. . . .

. . . .

. . . .

. . . .

. . . .

. . . .

2:1 Travel writing texts and preferences – dream holiday design

Reflect on your best and worst holidays and use these experiences to design your own dream holiday. Draw or write down ideas in the dream cloud below and then fill in the grid to identify your holiday preferences and the reasons for these.

Best holiday: ....
....
....

Worst holiday: ....
....
....

Holiday features	Preference(s)	Reasons
Destination		
Travel companions		
Accommodation		
Activities		
Food/drink		

Travel brochure writing

Introduction

In this lesson, students study a range of travel brochure extracts in order to identify the persuasive, linguistic and stylistic features that are commonly used in this type of text. They then create their own holiday brochure text aimed at a specific target audience, using their dream holiday plans from lesson 2:1.

Aims and objectives

- Explore the range, variety and overall effect on readers of literary, rhetorical and grammatical features used by writers of literary and non-literary texts.
- Create considered and appropriate effects by drawing independently on the range and variety of their own vocabulary, and by using strategies and resources to extend their available choices.

Starter (10 minutes)

Discuss the purpose and style of travel brochures: to persuade as well as to inform. Ask students to read through the four holiday brochure extracts on the task sheet and identify their target audiences and unique selling points.

Main phase (40 minutes)

- Introduce the learning objectives and feed back findings from the starter activity. Make sure that students are familiar with the following language features:
  — persuasive vocabulary (positive language that makes you want something);
  — the imperative (commands/instructions);
  — appealing facts/opinions (those that put a positive slant on the product).
- Students highlight these language features, using three different colours, and discuss their effects on the target audiences.
- Students then create their own piece of persuasive travel brochure writing (they can use their plans from their dream holiday design in the last lesson). They must try to include as many of the language features as possible.

Plenary (10 minutes)

Students swap their travel writing pieces and highlight each other's texts to identify persuasive writing features. Select the best examples and award a class winner.

Homework ideas

Ask students to visit a travel agents to source a brochure for a specific holiday destination or type of vacation for a particular target audience. Get them to look through the brochure and prepare a short presentation about its contents.

Make it easier!

Provide students with a template for their own travel brochure writing.

Make it harder!

Look at travel websites or authentic travel brochures to extend students' understanding of this genre.

2:2 Travel brochure writing

1. Read the holiday brochure extracts below and highlight key words and phrases that give clues about the holidays' target audiences and USPs (unique selling points).

Honeymoon bliss

Indulge in the holiday of your dreams to celebrate tying the knot. Choose from a range of luxurious resorts across the Caribbean, all providing private beaches and pools to guarantee the privacy and romance you deserve on your special break. Our award-winning spas will provide you with the ultimate pampering experience, while our á la carte restaurants will not disappoint.

Cruise of a lifetime

Treat yourself to this once-in-a-lifetime holiday and explore the beauties of the Mediterranean coastline. This two-week cruise will take in all the delightful tourist spots and provide you with a wide menu of activities on board the liner – you can choose to do as little or as much as you like! The well-equipped, comfortable cabins will provide you with all the comfort and facilities that you desire to make the ship a home from home.

Discover the magic of Christmas

Take your family on a magical adventure that they will never forget – a visit to Santa's Grotto in Lapland! Stay in a traditional chalet, ride across the snow on a chauffeur-driven sleigh and meet all of Santa's helpers and reindeers! The highlight of the trip: meeting Father Christmas and Mrs Claus and seeing your little darlings' eyes pop open on their guided tour of the toy factory. This is the best holiday to bring a sparkle to your festive break.

INVIGORATING ACTIVITY BREAKS

Get yourself into shape with an exhilarating walking holiday on the Greek island of Pathos. While burning off the calories, you will enjoy breathtaking views of the beautiful countryside. Aside from the daily hikes, you will have the opportunity to swim, fish and scuba dive. Your hotel will also have a range of gym equipment and aerobics classes on offer.

---

2. Highlight examples of the following language features used in the holiday brochure extracts:

   - Persuasive vocabulary

   - The imperative

   - Appealing facts/opinions

3. Now create your own persuasive brochure text for your own holiday design. Don't forget to create a title and try to include all of the linguistic features above.

Researching destinations

Introduction

In this lesson, students use their teamwork and research skills to find out as much information as they can about a designated holiday resort. They then use their findings to create an informative leaflet about the resort.

Aims and objectives

- Use a range of reading strategies to retrieve relevant information and main points from texts, distinguishing between fact and opinion where appropriate.
- Plan writing and develop ideas to suit a specific audience, purpose and task by adapting familiar forms and conventions.

Starter (10 minutes)

Make a list of the factors that people consider when booking a holiday, such as price, weather, activities. Try to come up with at least four and then, in groups, ask the students to prioritise the importance of these factors.

Main phase (40 minutes)

- Introduce the learning objectives and explain that students will be working in teams to produce an informative brochure for their designated travel resort.
- Give out location cards to groups and get students to designate research priorities for each member of the team, i.e. one student researches weather, another student finds out about local food and drink delicacies. The list generated at the start of the lesson should help students to identify research topics.
- Once students have found out information about their country, they need to create an informative page about their designated topic. These pages then need to be amalgamated to create an informative leaflet.

Plenary (10 minutes)

Groups self-assess their leaflets and write a learning journal reflecting on their experience of working together as a group for this project:
- How effectively did they delegate tasks?
- How successfully did they complete independent research?
- What is the quality of their product like?

Homework ideas

Ask students to use a computer to create a polished version of their leaflet, including images.

Make it easier!

Provide students with leaflets from tourist information centres to give them a text model to aspire to.

Make it harder!

Ask students to tailor the content and style of their leaflets to a specific target audience with a particular unique selling point for the given location.

2:3 Researching destinations

1. Consider what matters to you most on holiday and make a list of your priorities below in order, e.g. destination, weather, activities. Discuss your choices and compare with others in your group to come to a consensus.

   1. ....

   2. ....

   3. ....

   4. ....

2. In groups you will be researching one of the locations below and producing an informative leaflet about this country as a holiday destination. You need to divide up this task so that each of you is responsible for producing a page about a particular aspect of this resort, for example local delicacies. Delegate topics from the list of priorities above.

Croatia	Mexico	Japan	Zambia
Dubai	New Zealand	Alaska	Sweden
Russia	Belgium	Jamaica	Ireland

3. You will be researching your given topic about the country using a computer. Make notes while you are browsing the internet and use these to create a page of the leaflet. These pages then need to be compiled to produce a group leaflet that you will be peer-judging.

4. Now reflect on how effectively you have worked as a team by writing a learning journal for this lesson. Use the following headings to help you:

   • How effectively did you delegate tasks?

   • How successfully did you complete independent research?

   • What is the quality of your product like?

Presenting different perspectives

Introduction
In this lesson, students familiarise themselves with the terms objective, subjective and bias. They examine three different descriptions of the same location to identify different styles of language used before practising to adopt different writing perspectives in their own writing.

Aims and objectives
- Explain how linguistic concepts are related, and use the terminology in ways that help them describe and review language use.
- Select techniques and devices used by writers, and draw on a range of evidence, opinions, information and the purpose of the task, in order to develop a consistent viewpoint in their own non-fiction writing.

Starter (10 minutes)
Use dictionaries and prior knowledge to create definitions for the terms objective, subjective and biased. Share definitions and check understanding among the class.

Main phase (40 minutes)
- Introduce the learning objectives and explain that students will be exploring how language is used according to the writer's perspective.
- Ask students to read the three descriptions of Brittany and identify the different writing styles used (persuasive/factual/anecdotal). Students should use the terminology from the starter activity to explain the language on the task sheet.
- Students then need to create three different descriptions of their home town, demonstrating that they understand and can use the various writing styles they have learned about in this lesson.

Plenary (10 minutes)
Discuss which style of writing is most useful for a tourist. What are the merits and limitations of objective, subjective and biased accounts?

Homework ideas
Ask students to visit a tourist information centre to source material about the local area and consider whether they agree with the way in which it has been presented. Ask them to write a paragraph explaining their views.

Make it easier!
Model openings of town descriptions for students who would benefit from extra support.

Make it harder!
Ask students to write a blog about their home town demonstrating a biased perspective.

2:4 Presenting different perspectives

1. Write the definitions of the different words below and then read the three extracts about the region of Brittany in France.

   Objective: ....

   Subjective: ....

   Biased: ....

   > With one of the most spectacular coastlines in France, encompassing granite cliffs, rocky inlets, sandy bays and colourful fishing harbours, Brittany boasts a proud sea-faring tradition.

   > Brittany is a peninsula and because it is almost surrounded by water, its weather often changes. The western coast is often damp and misty, especially during the late autumn and early spring.

   > Leaving Brittany's coastal port of Roscoff we drove inland to the historic town of Morlaix and began our hunt for somewhere to stay. What a delightful and confusing town Morlaix turned out to be!

2. Decide what style of writing each text is written in, using the terms above, and explain your choices in the space provided below.

   A ....
   ....
   B ....
   ....
   C ....
   ....

3. Now on a speparate sheet of paper create three different descriptions of your own home town, in the style of the extracts above.

© Helena Ceranic, 2011. *Resources for Teaching English: 11–14.*

Holidays from hell

Introduction

This lesson gets students to write about negative holiday experiences. After reflecting on their own bad holidays and examining an example of sarcastic travel writing, students plan and write their own holiday from hell account.

Aims and objectives

- Trace the development of a writer's ideas, viewpoint and themes.
- Draw on some techniques and devices used by writers in order to develop distinctive character and voice in their own fiction.

Starter (10 minutes)

Ask students to think back to their own bad holiday experiences. They then make notes in the box on the task sheet provided and share examples among the class.

Main phase (45 minutes)

- Introduce the learning objectives and explain that students will be looking at some negative travel writing before writing about their own holiday from hell in a similar style.
- Read the extract on the task sheet and discuss the style of the piece – how does the author create a sarcastic tone? Identify language that helps to bring the experience to life.
- Students then plan their own holiday from hell account. They should use the planning grid to gather ideas for the content before starting to draft their own descriptive response. Encourage students to incorporate the following language devices:
  — sarcasm
  — attention to detail
  — sensory description
  — exaggeration

Plenary (5 minutes)

Students select a best sentence from their descriptions, with evidence of one of the devices above, to share with the rest of the class.

Homework ideas

Ask students to interview two friends to find out about their worst holiday experiences and then write a report about their findings.

Make it easier!

Watch the Bank Holiday episode of *One Foot in the Grave* (available on YouTube) as stimulus material for holiday from hell ideas.

Make it harder!

Challenge students to include imagery in their negative descriptions to make them more entertaining.

2:5 Holidays from hell

1. Think of the worst holiday you have even been on. Make a note of everything that went wrong in the box below.

2. Read the travel writing extract below. Highlight all the descriptive phrases that help to bring the experience to life for the reader.

In the last stint of a gruelling six-hour train journey I was day-dreaming about arriving at my hotel . . . I would take a hot shower, snuggle up in a fluffy dressing gown, relax on my soft king-size bed, plumped up by huge pillows, and watch something vacuous on TV while ordering a scrumptious meal from room service.

The reality of my hotel was more Hitchcock than Hilton. I soon discovered that 'The Grand Hotel' was named ironically; I was greeted by the peeling hotel facade and the miserable face of a spotty teenager chewing gum and talking animatedly on her mobile phone. When I was eventually paid some attention, the adolescent pushed a set of grubby keys towards me and grunted, 'Chef's off sick – there's a chip shop next door'.

Upon opening the door to my coffin-sized room, I discovered that the hotel's interpretation of 'ensuite' was a toilet in the corner of the room that looked as though it had never been acquainted with bleach. The decor had all the trademarks of a short-sighted colourblind designer, and through the gargantuan spider's web that stretched across the bed frame I spotted the stained bed sheets and the congealed hospitality tray.

My journey was going to have to be a bit longer; I was not going to spend another minute in this fusty, dirty, hell-hole of a hotel.

3. Now use your own experiences, ideas from the extract, and your imagination, to create a holiday from hell. Use the planning grid below to make notes about the horrific ordeal. Then write a detailed description of the holiday experience.

Journey	
Accommodation	
Food	
Service	
Weather	

Letters of complaint

Introduction

In this lesson, students explore the motivations for letters of complaint before evaluating examples. Students then plan ideas for their own version. They use material from lesson 2:5 to write a convincing and demanding letter to their holiday providers. This lesson also feeds into the speaking and listening debate in lesson 2:7.

Aims and objectives

- Understand the significance and importance of conventional standard English, the ways in which writers use non-standard forms in specific contexts for particular effects, and how to use standard and non-standard English when appropriate in their own writing.
- Draw on their knowledge of grammatical conventions to write grammatically accurate texts that are appropriate to the task, audience and purpose.

Starter (10 minutes)

Discuss the reasons why people write letters of complaint and ask students to list motivations on the space in the task sheet provided. Identify the features of an effective letter of complaint. What should the content, style and tone be like (polite, forceful, convincing, aggressive)?

Main phase (45 minutes)

- Introduce the learning objectives and explain to students that they will be writing letters of complaint based on the holiday from hell account that they produced last lesson.
- Read the two examples of complaint letters and identify their strengths and weaknesses. In pairs, discuss their degree of appropriateness in the following respects:
  — structure
  — formality
  — supporting detail
  — purpose and outcome
- Share observations. Students then plan content for their own letters of complaint based on their holidays from hell. Draft letters if there is time.

Plenary (5 minutes)

Discuss how direct you should be in a formal letter of complaint. Should you demand specific outcomes?

Homework ideas

Ask students to word process their letters of complaint using a formal letter layout.

Make it easier!

Download a letter of complaint template from the BBC *Watchdog* website for students to use to help them with their own letters.

www.bbc.co.uk/watchdog/consumer_advice/complain_sample_letters_pic.shtml

Make it harder!

Introduce ABTA (the Association of British Travel Agents) to students and explore consumer rights in relation to holiday bookings.

www.abta.com/consumer-services/

2:6 Letters of complaint

1. Consider why people write letters of complaint. Discuss ideas in pairs and try to write down at least four motivations below.

    1. ....
    2. ....
    3. ....
    4. ....

2. Read the two letters of complaint below and identify their strengths and weaknesses.

---

63 Applegate Lane
East Huntingford
Hampshire
HS8 4DJ

14 September 2009

Dear Mrs Bellingham,

I am writing to complain about the poor service that I experienced at your restaurant, Chez Antoine, on Friday 12 September.

My husband and I waited over 15 minutes to be seated even though we had pre-booked. We then had to wait a further 10 minutes before the waitress came to take our drinks order.

The service throughout the rest of the meal was equally slow and when our meal did eventually arrive, my order had been mixed up. While we waited for the correct meal to arrive, my husband's dish got cold.

I am very disappointed by our experience on Friday night. We are regular customers at your restaurant and have never experienced this level of poor service before. I would like some form of compensation to restore our faith in your establishment.

I look forward to your response.

Yours sincerely

Mrs Julia Crossley

---

14 Water Crescent
Banbury
CV3 8RJ

Dear Manager of Shoe City,

I bought a pair of trainers at your shop on Saturday. The guy that served me was an absolute idiot and didn't have a clue what he was doing. He was rude to me and was too busy chatting to his mate on the till to give me any proper attention. When I got home I found out that the idiot had given me two different sizes in the shoe box. I couldn't believe it! I mean how useless can one person be?! I want a proper pair of trainers – getting a matching pair isn't much to ask, is it mate? This guy needs to get the sack pronto.

Yours

Steve

---

3. Now plan your letter of complaint below. Consider the best way to start, develop and end your letter for maximum impact.

    Opening: ....

    Middle: ....

    End: ....

Watchdog debate

Introduction

In this lesson, students prepare for a debate about a holiday complaint dispute. They argue in role for a *Watchdog* special: 'Holidays from hell'. Students will be assessed on their ability to argue their case effectively and convincingly, and other members of the class will be involved in peer evaluation.

Aims and objectives

- Engage listeners' attention and interest by using a range of different verbal and non-verbal techniques.
- Listen carefully, ask pertinent questions and make suggestions in order to solve problems and test ideas.

Starter (10 minutes)

Introduce the term 'watchdog' and explore what kind of TV programme this is from prior knowledge and/or word association. Discuss the need for consumer rights programmes and share students' understanding of the genre.

Main phase (30 minutes)

- Introduce the learning objectives and explain lesson outcomes: to argue in role on the subject of holidays from hell. (If students have completed lessons 2:5 and 2:6 they will have already described a disastrous holiday and written a letter of complaint. If doing this lesson in isolation, students will need time to generate ideas.)
- Form groups of three or four and ask students to identify the best holiday from hell story to use as the subject of this debate. The roles to be assigned are:
  — TV presenter (chair)
  — unhappy customer(s)
  — representative from the holiday company
- Give students an opportunity to plan their contributions in role, decide on a running order and rehearse the debate (using the planning spaces on the task sheet provided).

Plenary (20 minutes)

Watch performances and get audience members to grade students.

Homework ideas

Ask students to research two other consumer watchdogs such as Ofsted and Ofcom and find out what responsibilities they have and how they function. They should produce a fact sheet with their findings.

Make it easier!

Show students clips from consumer programmes to familiarise them with this style of debate. There are video links on the BBC's website:

www.bbc.co.uk/blogs/watchdog/

Make it harder!

Break up groups for the plenary task. Ask students to improvise their debates in their various roles.

2:7 Watchdog debate

1. Select the best holiday from hell scenario, or use ideas from several students. Write a summary of the main issues and events in the box below.

> **Holiday from hell:**

2. Decide on roles for each member of the group (below) and then agree on a running order for the debate, i.e. who will introduce it? In what order will the different people be introduced?

TV presenter (chairing the discussion): ....

Angry customer(s): ....

Representative from the holiday company: ....

> **Running order:**

Peer evaluation

Choose to focus on someone who is playing the same role as you and make notes about their performance against the criteria below.

- Engages listeners' attention and interest by using a range of different verbal and non-verbal techniques.

- Listens carefully, asks pertinent questions and makes suggestions in order to solve problems and test ideas.

Being economical with the truth

Introduction

In this lesson, students explore how persuasive travel writing can give a biased view of holiday resorts in order to entice customers to go there. They examine the concept of 'being economical with the truth' and identify examples of this kind of practice. They then practise the skill of turning a negative description into a positive one.

Aims and objectives

- Use inference and deduction to explore layers of meaning within a text.
- Draw on a repertoire of linguistic and literary techniques, and select those most appropriate for creating specific effects in their own writing.

Starter (10 minutes)

Introduce the term 'being economical with the truth' and ask students to guess the meaning of this phrase (putting a positive spin on the facts). Talk through the example on the task sheet; explore how writers use vocabulary selectively to give a positive spin on a negative scenario.

Main phase (40 minutes)

- Introduce the learning objectives and explain that students will be practising the skill of turning negative description into positive, as is commonplace in persuasive writing.
- Ask students to work out the implicit meaning of the other examples on the task sheet by writing the implied meanings of the sentences that have been made to sound positive:

  This complex of apartments is part of an exciting renovation project.
  The resort is a building site and the apartments haven't finished being built yet.

  The beach has an interesting and unusual texture.
  The beach is uncomfortable to sit on; it is made up of stones and shingle.

- Students then read through the description of Newmarket, identify all the negative features and modify the language used to turn this into a piece of positive, persuasive description.

  For example:

  Any visitor to Newmarket can experience the town's famous racing heritage. The equine way of life is embraced by the whole town; you cannot escape the truly unique atmosphere that the racing tradition boasts.

Plenary (10 minutes)

Compare students' text transformations and identify the most authentic and skilful use of language for effect within the class.

Homework ideas

Ask students to write an honest, warts-and-all description of their home town, pointing out all its not-so-glamorous features.

Make it easier!

Share images of holiday destinations that give contrasting depictions of their locations, e.g. rainy and crowded versus sunny and tranquil.

Make it harder!

Students generate two more examples of being economical with the truth, giving positive statements and their negative translations.

2:8 Being economical with the truth

1. What do you think this phrase means? Write your ideas in the space provided.

   Being economical with the truth:. . . . .

2. Look at the example of how a negative reality has been made to sound like a positive asset. Complete the remaining boxes below by working out the implied meaning behind the phrase.

   > The resort is conveniently situated near to the airport.
   >
   > *You won't be able to sleep at night due to the constant sound of planes taking off overhead.*

   > This complex of apartments is part of an exciting renovation project.
   >
   > . . . .

   > The beach has an interesting and unusual texture.
   >
   > . . . .

3. Now read the description of the racing town of Newmarket below. Identify all the negative features and think of alternative positive phrases that will make these sound like appealing facets of the town. Write your substitued description in the box below.

   > Newmarket: a town that reeks with the revolting stench of horse manure. Everywhere you go you are confronted with some kind of equine paraphernalia; even the town's fast food outlets are littered with novelty horse shoes and starting blocks!
   >
   > When you are not trying to contend with tasteless statues of the things, you end up getting stuck in huge queues of traffic waiting to pass a troop of horses on the road – have jockeys never heard of riding on fields?!
   >
   > There's not much else going on in the town. The high street is filled with tacky pound shops and rough pubs; after 8pm the streets are heaving with drunken larger louts and girls in mini-skirts.
   >
   > Thinking of visiting Newmarket? Do yourself a favour and miss the junction on the A14.

Spice up your city

Introduction

In this lesson, students create an advertising campaign convincing tourists to visit their home town/city/village. They rebrand their location and target a particular target audience. In groups, students produce a persuasive series of posters and present a pitch aimed at the local tourist board to convince them of their plans.

Aims and objectives

- Experiment with different ways of presenting texts, drawing on a range of modes, formats and media with the needs of the reader in mind.
- Select the most appropriate way to structure speech for clarity and effect, taking into account task, audience, purpose and context, and the range of supporting resources available.

Starter (10 minutes)

In groups, students generate a list of positive features about their town/city/village on a spider diagram, including such things as shopping facilities, open green spaces and good choice of restaurants. Then they consider what types of people would appreciate these features, i.e. young families/sports fanatics/couples.

Main phase (30 minutes)

- Introduce the learning objectives and outcomes: to create a marketing campaign to advertise your town/city/village to a specified target audience. Tell students that they will be working in groups to devise marketing posters and create a persuasive pitch to present to the local tourist board.
- In groups, students decide on roles: who will be responsible for the posters and who will write the pitch? They must agree on a specific target audience and a unique selling point for the town and then generate a marketing slogan.
- In pairs, or individually, students work on designated responsibilities and prepare to present materials and pitch to the rest of the class. Assign students with a specific time limit, depending on how many groups need to perform.

Plenary (20 minutes)

Perform pitches and present posters to the class, in role as members of the tourist board and local council. Get students to grade each other's campaigns.

Homework ideas

Ask students to design a series of marketing materials to advertise and promote their home town, such as a bookmark, tea towel or fridge magnet.

Make it easier!

Watch an excerpt from the BBC's *The Apprentice* episode where contestants were charged with the task of rebranding Margate with a similar marketing brief.

www.bbc.co.uk/apprentice/episode-extras/episode/ep_400009.shtml/

Make it harder!

Ask students to create a pitch for a TV advert as part of their marketing plans.

2:9 Spice up your city

1. Generate a list of positive features about your town/city/village.

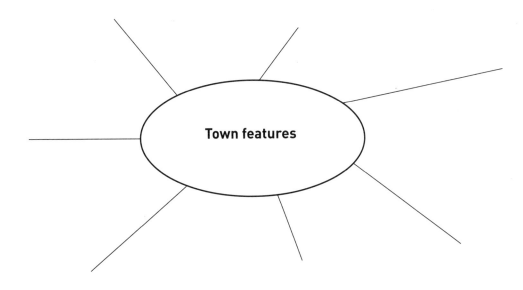

Town features

2. Now discuss your marketing campaign and note down your decisions in the boxes below.

> Target audience

> Unique selling point(s)

> Marketing slogan

> Poster design ideas

> Persuasive pitch ideas

Describing a cityscape

Introduction
In this lesson, students revise imagery techniques and focus on ways of structuring description. They then plan and write their own piece of sensory description focusing on a busy cityscape, demonstrating the use of linguistic and structural devices for effect.

Aims and objectives
- Use a range of cohesive devices with audience and purpose in mind, drawing on experience of how writers develop and connect ideas within and between paragraphs.
- Explore the range, variety and overall effect on readers of literary, rhetorical and grammatical features used by writers of literary and non-literary texts.

Starter (10 minutes)
Ask students to read and compare the two extracts on the task sheet and identify effective description. Discuss and identify the literary techniques used, e.g. personification (the tower is 'peeping slyly'), adjectives ('gruff', 'old') and effective vocabulary ('chattered').

Main phase (40 minutes)
- Introduce the learning objectives and outcomes: to produce a piece of effective description of a cityscape that demonstrates good use of structural and linguistic devices.
- Students choose one of the cityscapes options on the task sheet. Discuss different strategies for structuring description, as outlined on the task sheet, and their relative merits:
  — Paragraphing by sense (describe a different sense in each paragraph).
  — Zoom in/out in each paragraph (describe features as you get closer or further away from the focal point in the scene).
  — Pan across (describe different features in each paragraph as you visually sweep across a scene).
- Students select the structural method that they will use for their description and make notes in the planning boxes provided.
- Students write their description, following their plan and using at least two of the literary techniques identified in the starter activity.

Plenary (10 minutes)
The students swap descriptions with a partner and underline the other's use of linguistic devices. Share examples with the rest of the class and guess selected locations based on the description.

Homework Ideas
Ask students to create a description of a quiet and serene setting using the same literary techniques.

Make it easier!
Circulate a range of images of cityscapes for students to use as stimulus material for their writing.

Make it harder!
Ask students to include all of the literary devices identified in the starter.

2:10 Describing a cityscape

1. Read the two extracts below. Apart from being longer, why else is the second text a better piece of writing? Highlight words and phrases that are evidence of effective description.

A loud bell was ringing in the church tower.

The ancient tower of a church, whose gruff old bell was always peeping slily down at Scrooge out of a gothic window in the wall, became invisible, and struck the hours and quarters in the clouds, with tremulous vibrations afterwards as if its teeth were chattering in its frozen head up there. The cold became intense.

2. Make a list of linguistic devices used in the Dickens extract:

....

....

....

....

3. Select one of the city landscapes below for your descriptive task:

Piccadilly Circus, London	Central Park, New York
Amazonian rain forest	Eiffel Tower, Paris
Sydney Opera House	African safari

4. Look at the different planning structures for descriptive writing tasks and choose one of them for your task.

Senses	Zoom in/out	Pan across

Mystery customer report

Introduction

In this lesson, students revise the colon and semi-colon. They consider tourist ratings and reflect on examples of good customer service. In the guise of an inspector, they write a report about a real or imagined stay at a hotel and use this as an opportunity to apply a range of punctuation in an appropriately formal style.

Aims and objectives

- Draw on the full range of punctuation, including colons and semi-colons, to clarify meaning, aid cohesion and create a variety of effects.
- Draw on knowledge of how and why writers use varying degrees of formality and informality to make appropriate choices of style and register in their own writing.

Starter (10 minutes)

Students read the one star rating criteria and identify the colon and semi-colons used. Through deduction and discussion of prior knowledge, students write down the purpose that these pieces of punctuation serve in the text (a colon introduces a list, a semi-colon separates longer items in a list).

Main phase (40 minutes)

- Introduce the learning objectives and lesson outcomes: to produce a report on a hotel, commenting on the facilities in an appropriate register and also demonstrating an accurate use of a range of punctuation.
- Students complete activities 2 and 3 on the task sheet, using the examples to help them to use semi-colons in their own writing.
- Students then compile a report in role as a hotel inspector. They should use the provided headings to help them to structure their writing and should incorporate sentences using both colons and semi-colons accurately.

Plenary (10 minutes)

Peer-review inspection reports with a focus on register and punctuation usage.

Homework ideas

Ask students to review and compare the websites of three different hotel chains:

www.holidayinn.co.uk

www.hotelduvin.com

www.marriott.co.uk

Make it easier!

Get students to watch a clip from Channel 5's *Hotel Inspector* shown on YouTube to give them an idea about how to comment on facilities in their reports.

Make it harder!

Challenge students to use specialist terminology in their hotel report with reference to the star rating criteria:

www.fweb.org.uk/dean/visitor/accom/symbols.html/

2:11 Mystery customer report

1. Read the criteria for one star hotel accommodation below and highlight the use of colons and semi-colons. Explain what purpose each type of punctuation serves in the text.

   Colon (:) ....

   Semi-colon (;) ....

   > At a one star hotel you will find: practical accommodation; a limited range of facilities and services; a high standard of cleanliness throughout; friendly and courteous staff; restaurant/eating area open for breakfast and dinner; alcoholic drinks served in a bar or lounge; 75% of bedrooms with ensuite or private facilities.

2. Now create your own list of requirements for the features you would expect to find in a good quality hotel. Don't forget to use a colon and semi-colon in your writing.

3. Think of an example of good accommodation and customer service you have experienced while on holiday (use your imagination if you can't think of an example). Complete the sentences below using semi-colons to join linked statements as per the first two examples.

   The waiters were exceptionally good; they regularly checked whether we needed anything.

   Our room was spotless; we could have eaten our dinner off the floor.

   The view from our room was spectacular; ....

   The leisure facilities were great; ....

   The breakfasts were amazing; ....

4. Now imagine that you are a hotel inspector and you have been asked to write a report on the accommodation that you have stayed in. You need to address the following features and use a suitably formal style of language in your report. Don't forget to use colons and semi-colons in your writing to demonstrate that you can use a range of punctuation accurately.

   - Accommodation and bathroom facilities

   - Cleanliness

   - Customer service

   - Eating and drinking facilities

   For homework, review the following hotel chain websites and write a paragraph comparing them.

   www.holidayinn.co.uk   www.hotelduvin.com   www.marriott.co.uk

Rough guides

Introduction

In this lesson, students explore the content and style of rough guides. They consider readers' motivations for choosing this style of travel writing, before examining an extract. Students then employ this style of writing in their own rough guides that they produce about their school.

Aims and objectives

- Explore how different audiences choose and respond to texts.
- Plan writing and develop ideas to suit a specific audience, purpose and task by adapting familiar forms and conventions.

Starter (10 minutes)

Introduce the title 'rough guides' and prompt students to consider what kinds of travel writing texts fall into this genre. Discuss the answers to the following questions:

- Who writes rough guides?
- Who reads rough guides?
- How does the style and content of rough guides differ from travel brochures?

Main phase (40 minutes)

- Introduce the learning objectives and lesson outcomes: to write a rough guide to the school in the style of the text they are about to study.
- Ask students to read the extract from *The Rough Guide to Italy*. Students should annotate the text to identify the style of language used and the kind of information given to the reader (advice, local knowledge, reassurance). Share observations.
- In groups, students generate topics that they would include in a rough guide to their school. Designate a different topic to each group member and ask students to write a paragraph on their given topic. Remind students of the need to be honest and helpful in their rough guides.

Plenary (10 minutes)

Compile rough guide paragraphs. Write an introduction to the collective text as a group.

Homework ideas

Ask students to write a mini rough guide for a city or country that they have visited on holiday.

Make it easier!

Get students to explore the Rough Guides website (www.roughguides.com) and read extracts to gain a better understanding of the writing style for this type of text.

Make it harder!

Explore travel review websites such as www.tripadvisor.co.uk and consider the pros and cons of relying on web blogs as opposed to published travel writers.

Note: The online task sheet does not contain the extract from *The Rough Guide to Italy*.

2:12 Rough guides

1. Try to answer the following questions in discussion with other members of the class.

   - What is a rough guide?

   - Who writes rough guides?

   - Who reads rough guides?

   - How does the style and content of rough guides differ from travel brochures?

2. Read the extract from *The Rough Guide to Italy* below and annotate language features and types of information given to the reader, such as advice, local knowledge, reassurance.

> Despite what you hear about the Mafia, most of the crime you're likely to come across in Italy is of the small-time variety, prevalent in the major cities and south of the country, where gangs of *scippatori* or "snatchers" operate. Crowded streets or markets and packed tourist sights are the places to be wary of: *scippatori* work on foot or on scooters, disappearing before you've had time to react. As well as handbags, they whip wallets, tear off visible jewellery and, if they're really adroit, unstrap watches.
>
> You can minimise the risk of this happening by being discreet: don't flash anything of value, keep a firm hand on your camera, and carry shoulder-bags, as Italian women do, slung across your body. It's a good idea, too, to entrust money and credit cards to hotel managers. Never leave anything valuable in your car and try to park in car parks on well-lit, well-used streets. On the whole it's common sense to avoid badly lit areas completely at night and deserted inner-city areas by day. Confronted with a robber, your best bet is to submit meekly; it's an excitable situation where panic can lead to violence – though very few tourists see anything of this.

This extract from *The Rough Guide to Italy* 9/e by Rob Andrews, Ros Belford, Jules Brown and Jonathan Buckely (Rough Guides, 2009) Copyright © Rough Guides 2009 is reproduced with the permission of The Penguin Group.

3. Now consider what you would include in a rough guide to your school, aimed at students who have recently joined. What information, advice and tips would you include? Decide on a range of topics and note them down in the circles below.

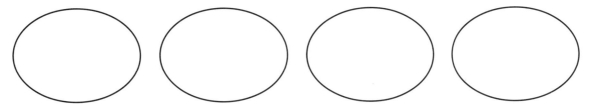

4. Write one of these topics into an informative paragraph following the stylistic conventions you identified in the rough guide above.

Identifying audience, purpose and style

Introduction

In this lesson, students identify the features of different text types and writing styles. Students examine a variety of texts and consider various content, style and formality in relation to audience and purpose.

Aims and objectives

- Analyse how meaning is conveyed differently according to the form, layout and presentation selected by the writer for specific purposes.
- Analyse and exemplify the way that forms and varieties of English used by speakers and writers can be influenced by context and purpose.

Starter (10 minutes)

Students write a definition of a letter, an email, a text message and a postcard and answer questions:

- Why are they written? (to inform/keep in touch/ask something)
- Who are they written for? (friends/family/businesses)
- How are they similar/different? (purpose/level of formality)

Main phase (40 minutes)

- Introduce the learning objectives and lesson task: to read a variety of different texts and identify their different audiences, purposes and styles.
- Students read through the four texts on the task sheet and discuss their form and content. They then make notes in their books, answering the following questions:
  — Who has written the text?
  — Who is the text addressed to?
  — Why has the text been written?
  — What is the style of language and sentence structure like in the text?
- Students then select a quotation from each text as evidence of the content and style of the text.

Plenary (10 minutes)

Students write a paragraph explaining how the style of language and sentence structure differs according to the formality of the text, using examples to support points.

Homework ideas

Ask students to find two different styles of text that are intended for two different audiences and purposes and write a comparative explanation of them.

Make it easier!

Complete the questions together for the first two texts to model how to respond.

Make it harder!

Turn the text message into Standard English and discuss the merits and drawbacks of using abbreviated language forms.

3:1 Identifying audience, purpose and style

A

Mr and Mrs Grantham
3 Potters Lane
Nottingham
NG14 5SL

Dear Mum and Dad,

Just to let you know that we are having a fab time in Sardinia . . .

The views here are stunning and we have been on lots of lovely walks. The weather has been gorgeous and the fresh fish here is delicious. Charlie has made lots of new friends at the kids' club. Wish you were here!

Love from Lynne, James and Charlie xx

B

TIIII _abc
11.21
New text message
906/01

To:
Karl mob
[=44897 4665241]

Text:

Hey m8, do u fancy goin 2 c a film 18r? We cud meet outside Burger King @ 3 and c wots on?

C

Roberts, Palmer & Co.
5 Broadway
Oxford
OX2 5EP

Ref: ML/GP40216

15 Drury Lane
Fowlsmere
Oxfordshire
OX7 3DH

17th July 2009

Dear Miss Phillips

Re. Purchase of 22 Lime Street, Oxford

I am writing to inform you that contracts have now been exchanged for the purchase of 22 Lime Street. Please find corresponding documentation herewith.

Completion is scheduled to take place on 1 August. Please make an appointment with my secretary to sign the relevant paperwork in the next week.

Yours sincerely,

pp M.Leighton

Geoffery Palmer (Partner)

D

Hi Aimee,

I've just heard your exciting news – congratulations!!

How did Rob propose? Have you set a date yet? So many questions . . .!

Congratulations!

I can't wait to see you to find out all of the gossip over a class of celebratory bubbly!

I'm so happy for you both.

Lots of love and hugs,

Carlie xxxx

Lottery writing tasks

Introduction

In this lesson, students imagine that they are lottery winners and write a variety of different texts to inform friends, family and employers of their win. Students practise adapting their writing form and style according to the audience it is intended for.

Aims and objectives

- Plan different types of writing and develop ideas by drawing on the ways in which forms and conventions can contribute to the overall impact and effectiveness of texts.
- Understand the range of formal and informal styles used by writers, and ways to deploy them appropriately in their own writing to enhance and emphasize meaning and create a wide range of effects with task, purpose and reader in mind.

Starter (10 minutes)

Ask students to imagine that their six lotto numbers are called out in the National Lottery draw on Saturday. In pairs, get them to discuss the following questions with their partners:

- How would you feel?
- Who would you contact?
- What would you plan to do with the money?

Discuss answers with the rest of the class.

Main phase (45 minutes)

- Introduce the learning objectives and explain that students will be producing three different styles of text informing people about their lottery win: a text message to a friend; an email to a relative; a letter of resignation to an employer.
- Students plan the content and style for the three texts on the accompanying task sheet. Share ideas, especially for the letter of resignation – what kinds of things might you want to tell your boss about your time at work and your reasons for leaving?
- Students then produce the texts, paying attention to an appropriate use of Standard English for their audience.

Plenary (5 minutes)

Consider how audiences would react to these texts – discuss what kind of response you would expect from the friend, relative and boss.

Homework ideas

Ask students to word process their letter of resignation using formal presentation devices.

Make it easier!

Recap the presentational features of a formal letter – make sure that students know where addresses should go and the rules regarding 'yours sincerely' (when addressed to a specific person) and 'yours faithfully' (when addressed 'Dear Sir/Madam').

Make it harder!

Write an email response advising a relative how to cope with their lottery win.

3:2 Lottery writing tasks

1. Imagine you have chosen the following winning lottery numbers, bagging £6.5 million!

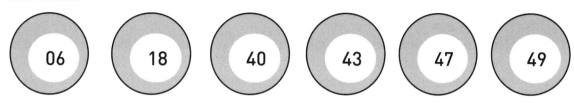

Discuss your answers to the following questions about your win:

- How would you feel?

- Who would you contact?

- What would you plan to do with the money?

2. Now plan how you are going to tell people about your good news. You are going to produce the following texts:

- text message to a friend

- email to a relative

- letter of resignation to your boss

Make notes about the content and style in the boxes provided below.

Text message to a friend

Email to a relative

Letter of resignation to your employer

3. Now write the texts on a separate piece of paper.

Letter to space

Introduction

In this lesson, students revise noun types, with a particular emphasis on common and proper nouns. They then plan the content for a letter to space, informing alien life forms about how life works on Earth. Students will need to be very explicit and detailed in their explanation in order to fulfil the requirements of the designated audience and purpose.

Aims and objectives

- Link their selection of ideas and planning choices explicitly to a clear sense of task, purpose and audience and the individuality of their own writing.
- Establish and sustain a clear and logical personal viewpoint through the analysis and selection of convincing evidence, opinions and appropriate information, and other techniques used by writers to meet the purpose of the task.

Starter (10 minutes)

Students recap noun types by thinking of examples of each and then sorting words on the task sheet depending on whether they are common or proper nouns (and therefore needing a capital letter).

Main phase (40 minutes)

- Introduce the learning objectives and outcomes: to write a letter to space informing alien life forms about what life is like on Earth. Discuss the fact that students will need to be very explicit in their explanation.
- In groups, students discuss the topics that would be best to include in the letter to space, such as food, jobs, housing. They then fill in the planning grids with decided topics and details to include in each paragraph.
- Students write the letter, remembering to explain each feature in detail for the benefit of the target audience.

Plenary (10 minutes)

Swap letters. Students underline words or phrases that need further explanation and clarification and then make the suggested alterations.

Homework Ideas

Ask students to create a poster advertising Earth as an ideal holiday destination for aliens.

Make it easier!

Model a paragraph with the class to exemplify how to write a detailed explanation.

Make it harder!

Turn a paragraph of the letter into a manual for aliens, instructing them on a particular aspect of human activity.

3:3 Letter to space

1. Look at the different noun types listed below and add two more examples to each type.

Common nouns: dog friend town ....

Proper nouns: Lassie Natalie York ....

Pronouns: he she it ....

Collective nouns: pack group cluster ....

Abstract nouns: jealousy love pride ....

2. Then sort the nouns listed below into the correct circle, depending on whether they are proper or common nouns. Remember to add a capital letter to proper nouns.

school   work

tesc   home

aliens   humans

london   space

earth

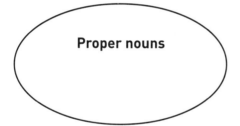

Proper nouns

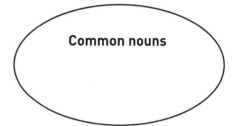

Common nouns

3. You are going to write a letter to space, informing alien life forms about life on Earth. Plan your paragraph topics in the grid below.

Topic	Details

Room 101

Introduction
In this lesson, students prepare for a speaking and listening presentation in which they persuasively argue for three of their hated items to be permanently placed in Room 101. They have to justify their choices effectively and be prepared to argue their case.

Aims and objectives
- Select from a wide repertoire of resources and ways of organizing and structuring talk to present information appropriately and persuasively for listeners in a range of familiar and unfamiliar contexts.
- Develop and choose effectively from a repertoire of verbal and non-verbal techniques which actively involve listeners.

Starter (10 minutes)
Introduce the concept of Room 101 from George Orwell's novel *Nineteen Eighty-Four*. Students create a list of items that irritate or annoy them and that they would like to see banished to Room 101 and then select the three that they feel most passionate about.

Main phase (45 minutes)
- Introduce the learning objectives and lesson outcomes: to present their chosen Room 101 items to the rest of the class and convince their audience to banish them.
- Students prepare to use a range of persuasive reasons and justifications for each of their chosen Room 101 items. Tell them to use prompts on the task sheet to help with this.
- Set up the classroom like a talk show. Students take it in turns to be interviewed by the programme host and present their hated items.

Plenary (5 minutes)
Members of the audience consider all of the objects that have been presented and select one item to be banished to Room 101 based on the persuasiveness of the speaker's presentation.

Homework ideas
Ask students to write a persuasive pitch to ban one of the following items from school:
- chewing gum
- mobile phones
- make-up

Make it easier!
Show a clip of the BBC show *Room 101* from YouTube to give students a sense of the show's format and style.

Make it harder!
Students have to argue for designated popular items, such as chocolate, to be banished.

3:4 Room 101

Think of three items/ideas/things (not people) that you would like permanently removed from the planet Earth.

You must think of valid reasons for their removal and explain in detail why the items/ideas/things cause you so much dislike.

You must present your ideas to the class for this speaking and listening assignment.

1. Write down your three chosen Room 101 items below.

   1. . . . .

   2. . . . .

   3. . . . .

2. Now use these prompt questions to help you to prepare for your presentation.

   - What is the first item you would like to banish to Room 101?

   - When did you first realise that you hated it so much?

   - Many other people will disagree with your choice. What would you say to make them change their minds?

   - What is the second item you would like to banish to Room 101?

   - What is it particularly that you hate about it?

   - Surely there must be at least one good thing about this item? Do you agree? Why?

   - What is the third item you want to banish to Room 101?

   - Room 101 is quite full now. I'm afraid only one item out of your three can fit in. Which one would you like it to be and why?

3. Having listened to lots of different presentations, which one item do you think deserves to go into Room 101 and why?

Big is beautiful

Introduction
In this lesson, students have the opportunity to develop their reading comprehension skills. After analysing the presentational devices used in an article, they will demonstrate their understanding of the text's argument and language effects. Discussion of the issues in the article could also be good preparation for the writing task in lesson 3:6.

Aims and objectives
- Use a repertoire of reading strategies to analyse and explore different layers of meaning within texts.
- Develop interpretations of texts, supporting points with detailed textual evidence.

Starter (10 minutes)
Ask students to discuss the title 'Big is Beautiful' in pairs. Get them to predict what the article they are going to read is about, and consider the connotations of this statement. Share interpretations and the issues relating to them, i.e. weight, obesity, anorexia.

Main phase (40 minutes)
- Introduce the learning objectives and lesson outcomes: to respond to a media text and demonstrate assured reading comprehension skills.
- Read the 'Big is Beautiful' article, pausing to underline key words and discuss the text's argument.
- Students complete the comprehension questions individually or in pairs.

Plenary (10 minutes)
Focus on the marks awarded per question and demonstrate how to achieve higher marks, i.e. including specific evidence and detailed explanation of effects.

Homework ideas

Ask students to research the condition bigorexia further and write some brief notes about it.

Make it easier!
Model answering the first comprehension question, using evidence from the text.

Make it harder!
Compare this article to the Wise Geek's entry about bigorexia:

www.wisegeek.com/what-is-bigorexia.htm/

Consider how the authorial voices of the two texts differ and the reasons for this.

3:5 Big is beautiful

Big is beautiful

You've heard of anorexia but what about bigorexia? Phoebe Marsh takes a look at the pathological preoccupation with 'bulking out'

Bigorexia, a condition also known as 'The Adonis Complex', is a term which is used to refer to men and women who train obsessively to build up their bodies.

In a society in which obesity is on the increase, regular exercise and taking pride in keeping fit should be seen as a good thing. However, like everything in life, it's only good in moderation.

There are numerous health risks involved with the compulsion to work out. Bigorexia spurs people to exercise even to the point of injury and those suffering from the disorder often take excessive amounts of anabolic steroids and proteins in order to 'bulk out'.

For bigorexics, exercise is not just a hobby – it becomes their life. They will often spend as much as three hours a day thinking about their muscles.

Bigorexics, like anorexics, have a drastic misconception of their body image. They consider themselves as puny, regardless of how muscular they actually are.

The disorder manifests itself in similar ways to anorexia.

Bigorexics exhibit dissatisfaction with their bodies, suffer from regular mood swings, anxiety and eating disorders.

Although the disorder is largely unheard of, it affects one in every 500 to 1,000 individuals. *Science Today* enforces the seriousness of the condition: 'muscle dysmorphia is a valid mental disorder characterised by a pathological preoccupation with muscularity'. They state that it is a predominantly male disorder, which usually begins during adolescence.

Studies support the claim and show that male teenagers are showing increasing dissatisfaction with their bodies and are desperate to shed their boy-like image and become muscular.

An alarming number of school children are so desperate to obtain the 'perfect body' that they are turning to anabolic steroids to do so. In a recent survey conducted in Merseyside, three per cent of children, some as young as 15, admitted to taking steroids, making them the third most commonly offered drug after cannabis and ecstasy.

Although the use of steroids is legal, the drug could have

extremely detrimental effects on the body, especially when taken in high dosages during puberty. Potential long-term effects include liver and kidney failure, heart problems and dangerously low blood pressure. Females taking the drug may develop certain masculine features such as facial hair.

The advent of Bigorexia appears to be yet another consequence of our society's obsession with appearance. The world of advertising makes sure that we never feel content with our bodies. While some men and women spend their lives trying to get as tiny as possible, others want to get as big as possible; what's wrong with being average and healthy?

Why do a substantial amount of people feel the need to subject their bodies to an abnormal amount of exercise or consume an insufficient amount of food in order to achieve an unnatural appearance? If people have the self-discipline to torture their bodies in this way, it is a shame that they don't channel it into making sure that they live a healthy life and look after their bodies.

1. What is Bigorexia? (2 marks)

2. How does the writer use facts in the article? (3 marks)

3. What is the author's opinion on the disorder? (5 marks)

Under pressure

Introduction

In this lesson, students discuss the various pressures that teenagers have to deal with. In groups they identify the most influential issues that affect adolescents and then plan the content for an advice brochure aimed at teens. Students then produce a section of advice writing, demonstrating their ability to write sensitively for a specific audience and purpose.

Aims and objectives

- Move a discussion forward by developing and drawing together ideas arising from discussion.
- Understand the ways in which writers modify and adapt phrase and sentence structures and conventions to create effects, and how to make such adaptations when appropriate in their own writing.

Starter (10 minutes)

In groups, ask students to generate a list of the top five stresses and pressures that affect modern teenagers, such as examinations, relationships and peer pressure. Students will need to discuss their ideas in collaboration and come to an agreement.

Main phase (40 minutes)

- Introduce the learning objectives and lesson outcomes: to produce an advice text aimed at teenagers to help them cope with pressure and stress that they are experiencing.
- Recap the features of advice texts (sympathy, suggestions, reassurance) and ask students to identify the sample sentences on the task sheet that use an appropriate style of language and phrasing.
- In groups, students delegate different advice topics from their top five list to individuals or pairs.
- They then plan content ideas and recap stylistic conventions of advice writing.
- Students complete advice writing sections, maintaining a focus on audience and purpose.

Plenary (10 minutes)

Groups rejoin and collate their pieces of advice writing. They must agree on suitable headings and sub-headings to structure the text.

Homework ideas

Ask students to research the Connexions website (www.connexions-direct.com) and choose two topics (e.g. careers, relationships, health). They need to summarise the advice offered to teenagers about these particular areas of their lives.

Make it easier!

Show students a piece of sample advice writing to familiarise them with this text type. For example:

www.connexions-direct.com/index.cfm?pid=141&catalogueContentID=325/

Make it harder!

Ask students to change the target audience for their advice writing to stressed parents trying to cope with their teenage children.

3:6 Under pressure

1. In groups, discuss what pressures and stresses teenagers have to deal with and then agree on a top five. Note your choices down below.

   1. ....
   2. ....
   3. ....
   4. ....
   5. ....

2. Look at the sentences below. Which ones are good examples of advice writing, and why? Circle and annotate your selected sentences.

   Just get a grip – it's not the end of the world.

   Why don't you try speaking to someone you trust?

   You could use the internet to find lots of advice on how to cope with exam stress.

   Do exactly as I say and you will never be stressed again.

   Don't worry; most teenagers suffer from bouts of low self-esteem.

3. Write down the features of effective advice writing below. What kind of language and style is appropriate?

   ....
   ....
   ....
   ....

4. Now complete your advice writing, ensuring that you focus on the audience and the purpose of the text.

The Red Room

Introduction

In this lesson, students discuss the connotations associated with certain colours before reading an extract from H. G. Wells' *The Red Room* as an introduction to gothic fiction. They identify the descriptive features that help to create atmosphere and tension in the text and then design their own room to describe.

Aims and objectives

- Analyse in depth and detail writers' use of literary, rhetorical and grammatical features and their effects on different readers.
- Shape and affect the reader's response through conscious choices and in planned ways by selecting ambitiously from a wide and varied vocabulary for a range of tasks, purposes and readers.

Starter (10 minutes)

Ask students to write down the associations they have with the colours listed on the task sheet. Discuss what kind of connotations of literary genres they hold, e.g. black suggests mystery; pink connotes romance. Introduce the title of the short story, *The Red Room*, and invite students to share their predictions about the type of genre this text belongs to.

Main phase (40 minutes)

- Introduce the learning objectives and lesson outcomes: to read H. G. Wells' text in order to develop their own ideas for a piece of descriptive writing based on a place.
- Before starting to read the extract, introduce students to the term 'gothic fiction' and share any prior knowledge of its features, e.g. isolated settings; pathetic fallacy; the supernatural.
- Read the text together and pause to identify and discuss examples of descriptive phrases that help to create atmosphere and tension in the text.
- Students then return to their starter activity to select an alternative coloured room to write about. They create a back story to this room and plan ideas. For example, the white room might be located in an abandoned mental asylum, haunted by ghosts of past residents.

Plenary (10 minutes)

Students craft a few sentences of description of their room, using ideas and devices they discovered in *The Red Room* text.

Homework ideas

Ask students to complete their own room description using a range of literary devices to create the desired atmosphere.

Make it easier!

Watch extracts from Tim Burton's *Charlie and the Chocolate Factory* to get ideas for different room designs.

Make it harder!

Introduce students to another extract from a gothic text such as *Dracula* or *Northanger Abbey*.

Note: The online task sheet does not contain the extract from *The Red Room*.

3:7 The Red Room

1. Write down connotations of the colours below; consider what you associate them with. Make notes around the circles.

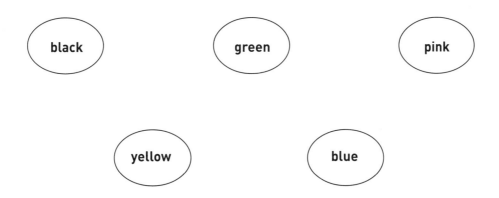

black

green

pink

yellow

blue

2. Read the extract below and identify phrases that help to create atmosphere and tension for the reader.

> And looking around that large shadowy room, with its shadowy window bays, its recesses and alcoves, one could well understand the legends that had sprouted in its black corners, its germinating darkness. My candle was a little tongue of flame in its vastness, that failed to pierce the opposite end of the room, and left an ocean of mystery and suggestion beyond its island of light. I resolved to make a systematic examination of the place at once, and dispel the fanciful suggestions of its obscurity before they obtained a hold upon me. After satisfying myself of the fastening of the door, I began to walk about the room, peering round each article of furniture, tucking up the valances of the bed, and opening its curtains wide. I pulled up the blinds and examined the fastenings of the several windows before closing the shutters, leant forward and looked up the blackness of the wide chimney, and tapped the dark oak panelling for any secret opening. There were two big mirrors in the room, each with a pair of sconces bearing candles, and on the mantelshelf, too, were more candles in china candlesticks. All these I lit one after the other. The fire was laid, an unexpected consideration from the old housekeeper – and I lit it, to keep down any disposition to shiver, and when it was burning well, I stood round with my back to it and regarded the room again. I had pulled up a chintz-covered armchair and a table, to form a kind of barricade before me, and on this lay my revolver ready to hand. My precise examination had done me good, but I still found the remoter darkness of the place, and its perfect stillness, too stimulating for the imagination. The echoing of the stir and crackling of the fire was no sort of comfort to me.

Taken from *The Red Room* by H. G. Wells. Reproduced with the permission of A. P. Watt Ltd on behalf of The Literary Executors of the Estate of H. G. Wells.

3. Now, on a separate piece of paper, plan your ideas for your own description of a particular room. Use your colour connotations to help you to generate ideas.

Car advert analysis

Introduction

In this lesson, students use their analytical skills to compare two different car adverts. Using suitable media terminology, they explain the specific messages and effects created by the two contrasting texts and justify their preferences with supporting details.

Aims and objectives

- Analyse how texts are shaped by audiences' preferences and opinions.
- Analyse a range of texts or language uses, drawing on terminology related to literary, linguistic and grammatical features.

Starter (10 minutes)

Ask students to think of a memorable television advert they have seen recently. Consider what strategies the advertisers have used to make an impact, for example, humour, celebrity endorsement, a catchy slogan. Share ideas with the rest of the class. Now ask students whether they can recall a car advert they have seen that they either liked or disliked and explain why.

Main phase (40 minutes)

- Introduce the learning objectives and lesson outcomes: to complete a comprehensive comparative analysis of two TV car adverts, reviewing their target audiences and media devices and commenting on their effects.
- Watch two car adverts on www.tellyads.com once through and discuss first impressions. Then watch several times, allowing students time to make notes on the task sheet provided and identify specific details from the adverts.
- Students then use their notes to write a detailed analysis of the two adverts. They should compare the two adverts throughout, rather than analysing one at a time. They may wish to use two boxes on the grid per paragraph, e.g. make/model and narrative; characters and settings. The final paragraph will then be a conclusion containing their preferences and opinions.

Plenary (10 minutes)

Ask students to decide which advert is the most effective for its target audience. Discuss and ask students to justify their claims with reference to their analysis.

Homework ideas

Ask students to analyse an additional car advert and incorporate this analysis into their essay.

Make it easier!

Model the analysis technique using students' suggestions and ideas from their notes.

Make it harder!

Ask students to recommend, in their conclusion, changes that could be made to the adverts to improve them.

3:8 Car advert analysis

	Car advert 1	Car advert 2
Make and model		
Narrative *What's happening*		
Characters *Age? Gender? Social class?* *Lifestyle?*		
Settings *What kind of landscape?*		
Sound *Voice-over? Music? What are* *they like?*		
Words *Is there any text on screen?*		
Unique selling point *What is the car's special* *appeal?*		
Target audience *Who do you think the ad is* *being aimed at? Why?*		
Rating/10 *How effective do you find the* *advert?*		

Car target audiences

Introduction

In this lesson, students develop their understanding of target audiences and unique selling points by matching up consumer needs to different vehicles. They write responses advising buyers before developing their own designs for a dream car. In groups, they work collaboratively to develop a concept for a new car aimed at a specific audience.

Aims and objectives

- Recognize strengths and identify areas for development in their own and others' contributions.
- Write fluently and sustain standard English in wide and varied texts and contexts, and for a range of purposes and audiences.

Starter (10 minutes)

In groups, ask students to discuss their car preferences from the list of cars on the accompanying task sheet. Feed back and discuss popular qualities and how these relate to the circumstances of the buyer, e.g. someone who lives in the countryside may be more likely to choose a 4 × 4 vehicle.

Main phase (40 minutes)

- Introduce the learning objectives and lesson outcomes: to match up cars to their target audiences and unique selling points before designing their own dream cars for a specified audience.
- In groups, students read the scenario cards and discuss the needs of the buyer depicted. They then decide on a suitable car for each customer and each write a response to one of the texts, advising the consumer on what car to buy. Students need to make sure that their writing sounds professional and knowledgeable and that they use Standard English to communicate their advice.
- Students then work together to design a concept for a new car. They need to decide on a specific target audience and price range for their product using the planning sheet, and plan design features and gadgets for their dream car design.

Plenary (10 minutes)

Split up groups and get them to explain their concepts to peers within other groups. This will help students to evaluate the quality of each other's designs.

Homework ideas

Ask students to research a particular make and model of car using the internet or a brochure. They should then write a paragraph explaining who it has been marketed at and how they can tell.

Make it easier!

Provide pictures of specific vehicles for students to choose from when completing the matching-up task.

Make it harder!

Encourage students to use specialist terminology in their advice writing.

3:9 Car target audiences

1. Given the choice, which one of the following cars would you want to drive when you are older? Discuss your reasons with others in your group.

Smart car	Porsche 911	Range Rover	Audi A3
Mercedes A class	Ford Focus	Mini Cooper	Citroen Saxo

2. Read the scenario cards below and discuss each customer's needs. In your groups, decide which car you would recommend that they should buy, based on the information you have about their lifestyle and interests.

> Carlie is a successful solicitor. She is a partner in a law firm and needs a car to get to various meetings. She sometimes has to take clients out so wants a car that is a comfortable ride and looks professional.

> Shirley owns a firm of florists. She needs a car that she can use to make deliveries at work. The shop is in the middle of town so it needs to be easy to manoeuvre and park. It will only be used for work purposes.

> Daniel is a stay-at-home dad. He has two young children and needs the car to do the school run and other chores. He also needs to use the car for fishing trips with his friends and for taking the dogs out for a walk.

> Rob has just passed his driving test. He needs an affordable car that will be cheap to run. He wants something attractive that will impress his mates and will be nippy for his trips to and from university.

3. Write a response to one of the customers in the scenario cards, advising them what car you think they should buy and justifying your reasons. Make sure that your writing is suitably formal and professional in style.

4. Now, design a new concept for a car. In your groups, decide on your target audience and unique selling point and then sketch the vehicle and label it with special features.

Dream car pitch

Introduction

In this lesson, students use their dream car designs that they developed in lesson 3:9. In groups, they develop a persuasive pitch to present to the rest in the class in the style of the BBC programme, *Dragons' Den*. Students are judged on the quality of their teamwork and their speaking and listening skills.

Aims and objectives

- Use and adapt a range of conventions and forms of spoken texts in different contexts for different purposes.
- Respond to speakers and give constructive feedback, analysing skills, subject matter, intended listeners and the purpose of talk.

Starter (10 minutes)

Watch an extract from a *Dragons' Den* episode (www.bbc.co.uk/dragonsden) to familiarise students with the format of the programme, and discuss the ingredients of a successful pitch.

Main phase (45 minutes)

- Introduce the learning objectives and lesson outcomes: to produce a successful pitch for your dream car in groups.
- Direct students to designate specific roles for their group's presentation, e.g. graphic design, writing the persuasive pitch. Students develop their concept, ready to present a pitch to the rest of the class.
- Students perform their pitches. They need to make sure that: their speech is clear and persuasive; all members of the group have a chance to contribute; they are ready to respond to questions.

Plenary (5 minutes)

Evaluate the success of the various performances and judge a class winner of the dream car pitch.

Homework ideas

Ask students to create an advertising poster for their dream car.

Make it easier!

Provide scaffolding questions for students to use when writing their pitch, e.g.: Who is your car aimed at? What is the car's best feature? How much are you aiming to sell it for?

Make it harder!

Identify a few 'dragons' for each performance who will challenge the groups with difficult questions and comments.

3:10 Dream car pitch

In this lesson you are going to work in a team to pitch your dream car in a *Dragon's Den* style activity.

1. Consider the different aspects of your dream car that you may wish to include in your pitch – some ideas are listed below. Agree on your roles and responsibilities for your dream car pitch.

    - target audience

    - unique selling point(s)

    - cost to buy and run

    - special features

2. Now draft your section of the pitch in the box provided.

Why Spy?

Introduction

In this lesson, students explore the concept of reality television and discuss the reasons behind the prolific popularity of this media genre. After sharing their own examples and views of examples of these types of programmes, they read an opinion article on this topic and analyse the writer's viewpoint.

Aims and objectives

- Understand the ways in which writers modify and adapt phrase and sentence structures and conventions to create effects, and how to make such adaptations when appropriate in their own writing.
- Discuss their own and others' reading, take account of others' views of what they have read, express informed opinions and make recommendations.

Starter (10 minutes)

Introduce the title 'Why Spy?' and discuss students' predictions of the topic of the lesson based on this phrase. Introduce the topic of reality TV and ask students to generate a list of programmes that fit into this genre, with celebrities or regular people, on the task sheet.

Main phase (45 minutes)

- Introduce the learning objectives and lesson outcomes: to engage with an opinion article on this topic and demonstrate their comprehension skills.
- Read the 'Why Spy?' article, either as a class or individually, and pause to discuss the writer's viewpoint and use of language. Ask students to respond to the text – do they agree with the arguments presented in it?
- Students answer accompanying comprehension questions, using details from the text to support their answers.

Plenary (5 minutes)

Share responses to the questions and judge the quality of students' answers, based on their level of detail and explanation.

Homework ideas

Ask students to examine the websites of two different reality TV programmes such as *I'm a Celebrity . . .*, *How Clean is your House* or *Big Brother* and write a review of the sites explaining the shows' appeal.

Make it easier!

Model completion of comprehension answers, emphasising the need to include supporting textual evidence.

Make it harder!

Ask students to create additional comprehension questions about the text and then answer each other's questions.

3:11 Why Spy?

1. Make a list of television programmes that involve watching celebrities or real-life people's behaviour. What is the appeal of these types of shows? Discuss why they are so popular and make notes next to the names of the shows.

   . . . .

   . . . .

2. Now read the article, 'Why Spy?' that was written after the first series of *Big Brother* in 2000 and answer the accompanying comprehension questions.

Why Spy?

In the aftermath of the hugely successful *Big Brother*, Becky Porter asks why we became so fanatical about watching a houseful of strangers

What has been the most significant event of the summer? Concorde crashing? The fuel crisis? The kidnapping in Sierra Leone? Or perhaps Channel 4's *Big Brother*?

It appears to be a rather sad reflection of the nation's mentality that over the past few months millions of people have been glued to watching a group of complete strangers go about their daily business.

Why did we become hooked on this banal concept? While the likes of *Eastenders* and *Coronation Street* keep up their ratings with a cocktail of car crashes, weddings and affairs, the inhabitants of the *Big Brother* household concern themselves with the amount of money they have allocated for their weekly grocery shop.

It hardly seems like the recipe for a successful TV show, but it was just that. Millions of people tuned in daily to learn about the latest happenings in the Big Bro. household, choosing to stay in on a Friday night to discover who had been kicked out instead of going out and meeting up with their friends.

The fact that a large proportion of the country became frankly obsessed with the programme suggests that as a nation we are voyeuristic in nature. How else could you account for millions of people tuning in to watch a group of twenty-somethings lazing on sofas having a chat?

What the programme has proved is that it takes very little to become famous. The *Big Brother* contestants became celebrities overnight by merely existing and getting on with others in confined conditions. Meanwhile, hundreds and thousands of talented hopefuls enrol in drama schools and invest years of hard work in a desperate attempt to make it big.

The programme has also highlighted how easily morality can be shifted. Erect a series of cameras in your neighbour's house and garden in an attempt to watch their daily habits and you will more than likely end up in prison for breach of privacy. Meanwhile Channel 4 lock ten people in a house and surround them with a multitude of cameras and 'it's only a game show'.

Of course, the notable difference is that the contestants consent to being spied on. It's not surprising really: how else would ten random members of the public achieve such fame in a matter of weeks for simply being themselves?

---

3. Comprehension questions

   - What language devices have been used in the title?
   - What attitude does the writer have towards the success of the reality TV show?
   - What is claimed to be the show's appeal?
   - What does the writer think of 'overnight celebrities'?
   - Why do you think people want to be on the show?

Little Brother application

Introduction

In this lesson, students create their own application for a reality TV show. After reading and discussing the advertised entry requirements, students plan the content for their own application. They need to consider what kind of information and presentation style will be well received by the programme's producers. They then create their own video audition tape.

Aims and objectives

- Elicit a range of responses from the reader, having made a judgement about the effectiveness of specific linguistic and literary techniques in particular contexts or for specific tasks.
- Develop and sustain a variety of processes, narratives, performances and roles through the selection and adaptation of appropriate dramatic conventions, techniques and styles.

Starter (5 minutes)

Discuss people's motivations for applying to go on a reality TV programme and read the advert for *Little Brother* applications on the task sheet.

Main phase (45 minutes)

- Introduce the learning objectives and lesson outcomes: to prepare for a video audition tape for *Little Brother*.
- Explore what makes an effective audition tape, with reference to the guidance given in the advert. What kind of housemate are the producers looking for? Discuss in groups and generate success criteria.
- Students plan the content of their video using the boxes on the task sheet and when they are ready, film the 1-minute audition tapes.

Plenary (10 minutes)

Watch a range of audition tapes and rate them according to whether they meet the criteria generated earlier in the lesson.

Homework ideas

Ask students to imagine that they are the producer of *Big Brother*. They need to create ten interview questions that they would ask potential housemates.

Make it easier!

Watch previous audition tapes for *Big Brother* on YouTube to generate ideas about what makes a good housemate.

Make it harder!

Ask students to create a fictional persona and act in role for their audition tape.

3:12 Little Brother application

1. Read the advert below for a new twist on the popular reality show series.

Be on *Little Brother!*

Little Brother! starts this summer and for the first time ever, you can apply to be a housemate if you are under 18 years old. Successful applicants between the ages of 12 and 16 will be chosen by *Little Brother!* to audition in person.

In early February, you will need to complete *Little Brother*'s application form and upload a 1-minute video to introduce yourself. The sooner you get your application in, the better your chance of being spotted by *Little Brother*, so get a headstart by filming your video now.

Before you start work on your 1-minute masterpiece, check out the ground rules . . .

- At the start of your video you MUST say your first name (but NOT your surname) and that you want to audition for *Little Brother 2011*. So for example, if your name is Callum Smith, at the beginning of your video you would need to say: 'Hello, I'm Callum and I want to be a *Little Brother 2011* housemate.'

- Your video must not exceed 1 minute.

- No music or singing, no matter how good you think your voice is.

- Your video will appear online, so make sure you don't reveal anything you wouldn't want the world to see.

2. Having read the entry requirements for *Little Brother!*, you are now going to prepare your application for the teenage reality show. Use the planning boxes below to select relevant information about yourself to include in the application.

Family and friends

Background

Hobbies and interests

Skills and qualities

Annoying habits

© Helena Ceranic, 2011. *Resources for Teaching English: 11–14.*

Section 2   Addressing literary fiction

Dickens' life and times

Introduction

In this lesson, students share their prior knowledge of Charles Dickens before conducting research about the author and his historical context. Students use their research and note-making skills to source appropriate information. They then construct informative leaflets with a focus on text structure and presentation.

Aims and objectives

- Make relevant notes when gathering ideas from texts.
- Shape the overall organization, sequence and presentation of a text to convey ideas clearly and effectively.

Starter (10 minutes)

Introduce Charles Dickens and share prior knowledge of this literary icon:

www.bbc.co.uk/history/historic_figures/dickens_charles.shtml/

Students fill in the spider diagram on their task sheets, adding information gained from other members of the class.

Main phase (40 minutes)

- Introduce the learning objectives and lesson task: to research Charles Dickens' life and times in order to produce an informative leaflet about him.
- Students use search engines on the internet to find appropriate websites including information about Charles Dickens. They make notes in the boxes on their task sheet.
- Once students have gained sufficient information, they start to compose their leaflets; they could either do this by hand or on the computer in a program such as *Publisher*. They need to make sure that they use appropriate presentational devices, such as headings, bullet points and images, to make their text engaging.

Plenary (10 minutes)

Swap leaflets (students may have to swap places if they have been working on the screen) and evaluate the quality of information and presentation used.

Homework ideas

Ask students to play the Survive Dickens' London game on the BBC website (www.bbc.co.uk/arts/multimedia/dickens) to meet some of Dickens' famous characters and gain an insight into what it was like for street urchins living in Dickensian London. They should be ready to feed back their experiences to the rest of the class.

Make it easier!

Watch a short video clip about Charles Dickens' life on the BBC *Bleak House* website:

www.bbc.co.uk/drama/bleakhouse/animation.shtml/

Make it harder!

Ask students to include recommended websites in their informative leaflets.

4:1 Dickens' life and times

1. Write down any facts that you already know about Charles Dickens on the spider diagram below. Discuss knowledge with the rest of your group to build up information.

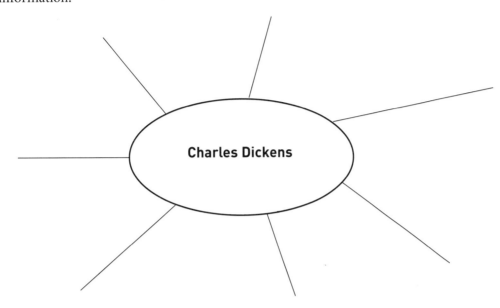

Charles Dickens

2. Use the internet to find further information about Dickens' life and times. Use the headings and the boxes below for note-making purposes.

Biography

Work

Society at the time

3. Once you have researched Charles Dickens, use this information to produce an informative leaflet about him. Use the headings above to help you to organise your text and include relevant and engaging images that you have found on the internet.

Dickensian London

Introduction

In this lesson, students explore the meaning of unknown words from a Charles Dickens extract using a range of strategies. They identify the author's use of sensory description before writing an analysis of Dickens' use of language for effect.

Aims and objectives

- Increase knowledge of word families, roots, derivations, morphology and regular spelling patterns.
- Identify and describe the effect of writers' use of specific literary, rhetorical and grammatical features.

Starter (10 minutes)

Discuss strategies for finding out the meaning of unknown words, e.g. using a dictionary; reading the word in context; looking for familiar word roots. Demonstrate with the class using the sentence: 'The ground was covered, nearly ankle-deep, with filth and mire'. Use the range of strategies to find the meaning of the word 'mire' (mud/sludge).

Main phase (35 minutes)

- Introduce the learning objectives and the Dickens text – an extract from *Oliver Twist*. Recap the meaning of sensory description with the class and direct them towards the activities on the accompanying task sheet.
- Students identify words that they do not understand in the extract and use the strategies discussed in the starter activity to find out their meanings. They then write down the definitions in the line spaces provided on the task sheet.
- Students then identify the author's use of sensory description within the extract and discuss its effect.

Plenary (15 minutes)

Students write a paragraph analysing Dickens' use of sensory description, selecting examples from the text to write about. Share and evaluate.

Homework ideas

Ask students to find out how many of Charles Dickens' novels included child labour and child poverty and make notes about this.

Make it easier!

Ask students to work in teams in order to find out the meanings of unknown words in the *Oliver Twist* text.

Make it harder!

Challenge students to use a thesaurus to include more complex vocabulary in their own descriptions.

4:2 Dickensian London

1. Read the extract from Charles Dickens' novel *Oliver Twist* below describing a cattle market. Highlight any words that you do not understand. Use a dictionary to find the meanings and annotate definitions in the spaces between the lines.

> It was market morning. The ground was covered, nearly ankle-deep with filth and mire; a thick steam, perpetually rising from the reeking bodies of the cattle, and mingling with the fog, which seemed to rest upon the chimney tops, hung heavily above. All the pens in the centre of the large area, and as many temporary pens as could be crowded into the vacant space, were filled with sheep; tied up to posts by the gutter side were long lines of beasts and oxen, three or four deep. Countrymen, butchers, drovers, hawkers, boys, thieves, idlers, and vagabonds of every low grade, were mingled together in a mass; the whistling of the drovers, the barking of dogs, the bellowing and plunging of oxen, the bleating of sheep, the grunting and squeaking of pigs, the cries of hawkers, the shouts, oaths and quarrelling on all sides; the ringing of bells and roar of voices that issued from every public-house; the crowding, pushing, driving, beating, whooping and yelling; the hideous and discordant din that resounded from every corner of the market; and the unwashed, unshaven, squalid and dirty figures constantly running to and fro, and bursting in and out of the throng; rendered it a stunning and bewildering scene that quite confounded the senses.

Taken from Charles Dickens' *Oliver Twist.*

2. Now reread the extract and highlight description that relates to the five senses, e.g. what you can smell, see, hear, touch or taste.

3. Consider what kind of atmosphere has been created by Dickens in this scene. Write a paragraph of analysis on a separate sheet of paper, explaining the effect that Dickens' language has on the reader, using examples from the text.

Miss Havisham

Introduction

In this lesson, students explore the character of Miss Havisham by looking at an extract from *Great Expectations*. After drawing a picture of her based on Dickens' description, students consolidate and extend their appreciation of the character by writing a report about her.

Aims and objectives

- Use inference and deduction to recognize implicit meanings at sentence and text level.
- Make a personal response to a text and provide some textual reference in support.

Starter (10 minutes)

Introduce the character of Miss Havisham from *Great Expectations* by telling the class that she is a jilted spinster (an unmarried woman who was stood up on her wedding day). Discuss and explain the words in this phrase and consider their connotations, especially in the context of expectations of women in Victorian England.

Main phase (40 minutes)

- Introduce the learning objectives and outcomes: to explore the character of Miss Havisham by looking at how she is described by Dickens in *Great Expectations*.
- Read the extract from the text, pausing to explore word meanings and impressions of the character. Students then draw a profile of Miss Havisham, based on the description, and label it with information from the text. Share and discuss character profiles.
- Students then complete a report on the character, noting down observations about her behaviour.

Plenary (10 minutes)

Share extracts from the reports and discuss recommendations that medical professionals would make for this character.

Homework ideas

Ask students to research Victorian attitudes and expectations towards women and marriage, and find out how Queen Victoria lived up to these. They should make notes to feed back to the rest of the class.

Make it easier!

Watch a clip on YouTube from David Lean's version of the text when Pip goes to visit Miss Havisham to gain more ideas and opinions about her character.

Make it harder!

Ask students to write their character commentary in the style of a psychiatrist's report.

4:3 Miss Havisham

1. Explore the meanings and connotations of the words below. What clues do these words give about Miss Havisham's character? Make notes around the words in the space provided.

jilted   spinster

2. Now read the descriptions of Miss Havisham in the extracts from *Great Expectations* below. On a separate piece of paper draw a picture of Miss Havisham based on the information given in the text, and label with details.

> No glimpse of daylight was to be seen in (the room).

> She was dressed in rich materials – satins, and lace, and silks – all of white.

> Her shoes were white. And she had a long while veil dependent from her hair, and she had bridal flowers in her hair, but her hair was white.

> Some bright jewels sparkled on her neck and on her hands, and some other jewels lay sparkling on the table.

> Dresses, less splendid than the dress she wore, and half-packed trunks, were scattered about. She had not quite finished dressing.

> I saw that the bride within the bridal dress had withered like the dress, and like the flowers, and had no brightness left but the brightness of her sunken eyes.

> I saw that the dress had been put upon the rounded figure of a young woman, and that the figure upon which it now hung loose, had shrunk to skin and bone.

> Her watch had stopped at twenty minutes to nine, and [. . .] a clock in the room had stopped at twenty minutes to nine.

> It was then I began to understand that everything in the room had stopped, like the watch and the clock, a long time ago.

3. Now write a report on Miss Havisham's character, based on the information you have uncovered from the text about her.

School reports

Introduction

In this lesson, students focus on how adjectives and adverbs can be used to add descriptive detail to statements. They study an extract from *Nicholas Nickleby* in which the school, Dotheby's Hall, is described. After focusing on how the negative vocabulary creates atmosphere in the text, students write the school's Ofsted report.

Aims and objectives

- Understand and make use of the most common terms used to describe language when referring to their own or others' language use.
- Develop their own viewpoint, drawing on evidence, opinions and the particular purpose of the task.

Starter (15 minutes)

Recap the word classes: verbs, adverbs and adjectives. Get students to elaborate on the statement 'the headteacher walked into the assembly hall' by experimenting with a range of verbs, adjectives and adverbs. Discuss how the choices affect the mood and context of the statement. Talk through the examples on the accompanying task sheet.

Main phase (40 minutes)

- Introduce the learning objectives and lesson outcomes: to explore a description of Dotheby's Hall in Dickens' *Nicholas Nickleby* before writing an Ofsted inspection report about the school.
- Students read the *Nicholas Nickleby* extract and highlight the adjectives used in the text. Discuss the effect that these words have on the description of the school; what kind of place does it seem to be?
- Students then use the Ofsted headings on the task sheet to write an inspection report about the school.

Plenary (5 minutes)

Discuss how modern schooling is similar to or different from the kind of establishment described in Dickens' text.

Homework ideas

Ask students to research corporal punishment and write a paragraph explaining their views on this outdated form of discipline.

Make it easier!

Show students an extract from a real Ofsted report, perhaps their own school's, to familiarise them with the style and format of this type of text.

Make it harder!

Ask students to include authentic Ofsted criteria in their reports. For ideas see:

www.ofsted.gov.uk/oxcare_providers/list/

4:4 School reports

1. Read the statement below and then make a list of adverbs, verbs and adjectives in the bubbles provided that could be inserted into the sentence to alter its meaning. Some examples have been provided for you.

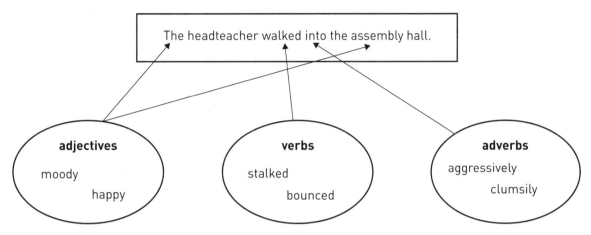

The headteacher walked into the assembly hall.

adjectives

moody

happy

verbs

stalked

bounced

adverbs

aggressively

clumsily

2. Now create three alternative sentences from a selection of your chosen words above. For example: The moody headteacher stalked aggressively into the happy assembly hall.

3. Read the description of Dotheby's Hall, a school in Dickens' *Nicholas Nickleby*. Highlight the writer's use of adjectives. Discuss the effect that these words have on the atmosphere and tone of the text.

> The place resolved itself into a bare and dirty room, with a couple of windows, whereof a tenth part might be of glass, the remainder being stopped up with old copy-books and paper. There were a couple of long old rickety desks, cut and notched, and inked, and damaged, in every possible way; two or three forms; a detached desk for Squeers; and another for his assistant. The ceiling was supported, like that of a barn, by cross-beams and rafters; and the walls were so stained and discoloured, that it was impossible to tell whether they had ever been touched with paint or whitewash.
>
> But the pupils – the young noblemen! How the last faint traces of hope, the remotest glimmering of any good to be derived from his efforts in the den, faded from the mind of Nicholas as he looked in dismay around! Pale and haggard faces, lank and bony figures, children with the countenances of old men, deformities with irons upon their limbs, boys of stunted growth, and others whose long meagre legs would hardly bear their stooping bodies, all crowded on the view together; there were the bleared eye, the hare-lip, the crooked foot, and every ugliness or distortion that told of unnatural aversion conceived by parents for their offspring, or of young lives which, from the earliest dawn of infancy, had been one horrible endurance of cruelty and neglect.

Taken from Charles Dickens' *Nicholas Nickleby.*

4. Now write an Ofsted inspection for Dotheby's school, based on the description above. Use the following headings to help you to structure your report:

- Facilities and accommodation

- Students' health and well-being

Pip in the graveyard

Introduction

In this lesson, students explore how Dickens uses language to create atmosphere and for dramatic effect. After analysing the encounter between Pip and Magwitch, with particular focus on sentence structure and punctuation, students predict events by writing the next section of the story.

Aims and objectives

- Understand how readers choose and respond to texts.
- Use punctuation accurately to clarify meaning and create effects in clauses, sentences and when writing speech.

Starter (15 minutes)

Read the short extract of description provided on the task sheet and discuss how Dickens creates a bleak and negative atmosphere. Explicitly discuss Dickens' use of complex sentences for effect. In their books, students write a brief paragraph of analysis (see instructions on task sheet).

Main phase (40 minutes)

- Introduce the learning objectives and lesson outcomes: to analyse Dickens' use of language and then continue the text with students' own predictions, based on what has happened so far in this scene.
- Students read the next episode from the text in which Magwitch confronts Pip. They then complete activity 4 on the task sheet – discussing the effect of Dickens' use of punctuation and sentence structure in the extract. Use t   his as an opportunity to revise grammatical terms.
- Students then predict the events in the text by writing the next two paragraphs (see prompts in the 'make it easier' section for students who need them).

Plenary (5 minutes)

Compare and evaluate predictions.

Homework Ideas

Ask students to compare the paragraph that they have written with the actual text and make notes on the similarities and differences between them.

www.online-literature.com/dickens/greatexpectations/1/

Make it easier!

Provide students with questions to support their writing:

- What does Magwitch do next?
- How does Pip feel?
- How does Pip escape from Magwitch?
- What does Magwitch ask Pip to do for him?
- How does Magwitch threaten Pip?

Make it harder!

Ask students to make sentence structure and punctuation an explicit focus of their writing.

4:5 Pip in the graveyard

1. Read the extract from chapter one of *Great Expectations* below and discuss how Dickens has created a bleak and negative atmosphere in the opening of his novel.

> . . . and that the dark flat wilderness beyond the church, intersected with dykes and mounds and gates, with scattered cattle feeding on it, was the marshes; and that the low leaden line beyond, was the river; and that the distant savage lair from which the wind was rushing, was the sea . . .

2. Write a paragraph analysing the author's use of language for effect. Which words are particularly effective?

3. Now read the next section of the chapter in which the central character, Pip, is confronted by a strange and aggressive stranger called Magwitch.

> 'Hold your noise!' cried a terrible voice, as a man started up from among the graves at the side of the church porch. 'Keep still, you little devil, or I'll cut your throat!'
>
> A fearful man, all in coarse grey, with a great iron on his leg. A man with no hat, and with broken shoes, and with an old rag tied round his head. A man who had been soaked in water, and smothered in mud, and lamed by stones, and cut by flints, and stung by nettles, and torn by briars; who limped, and shivered, glared and growled; and whose teeth chattered in his head as he seized me by the chin.
>
> 'O! Don't cut my throat, sir!' I pleaded in terror. 'Pray don't do it, sir.'
>
> 'Tell us your name!' said the man. 'Quick!'
>
> 'Pip, sir.'
>
> 'Once more,' said the man, staring at me. 'Give it mouth!'
>
> 'Pip. Pip, sir.'
>
> 'Show us where you live,' said the man. 'Pint out the place!'
>
> I pointed to where our village lay, on the flat in-shore among the alder-trees and pollards, a mile or more from the church.
>
> The man, after looking at me for a moment, turned me upside down, and emptied my pockets. There was nothing in them but a piece of bread. When the church came to itself – for he was so sudden and strong that he made it go head over heels before me, and I saw the steeple under my feet – when the church came to itself, I say, I was seated on a high tombstone, trembling, while he ate the bread ravenously.

Taken from Charles Dickens' *Great Expectations*.

4. Focus on Dickens' use of punctuation and sentence structure in this extract. What patterns do you notice and how do these affect the tone and atmosphere in the scene? Discuss the effect of the following in the extract, using examples to support your comments.

    *   exclamation marks
    *   the repetition of the connective 'and' in the second paragraph
    *   the use of complex sentences in the final paragraph

5. What do you think happens next? Write the next two paragraphs of the story, predicting the rest of this encounter between Pip and Magwitch.

What's in a name?

Introduction

In this lesson, students explain the notion of caricatures and stereotypes with a particular focus on the names that Charles Dickens chooses for his characters. They then devise their own caricature by personifying and describing an abstract noun.

Aims and objectives

- Use inference and deduction to recognize implicit meanings at sentence and text level.
- Use vocabulary precisely and imaginatively to clarify and extend meaning and create specific effects.

Starter (10 minutes)

Discuss the importance of names in Charles Dickens' texts and how the names he uses often give clues as to characters' personalities. Students choose three names from the list on the task sheet and predict the characters' traits from these.

Main phase (40 minutes)

- Introduce the learning objectives and lesson outcomes: students create their own caricature based on a specific abstract noun. They need to use vocabulary precisely in their description to bring their characters' features to life.
- Students need to revise the following terms: caricature, stereotype and abstract nouns (using dictionaries if necessary). They then select a noun from the choice on the task sheet and personify their chosen noun.
- After students have sketched and labelled an image of their devised character, they write a paragraph of description, using the prompts provided on the task sheet. They must use their imagination and a good selection of descriptive vocabulary in order to bring the character to life.

Plenary (10 minutes)

Students read out their descriptions, without revealing their characters' names. The other students have to guess the abstract noun that they have chosen, based on the clues given in the description.

Homework ideas

Ask students to create a collage for their given abstract noun using a range of images and colours to reflect its explicit and implicit meanings.

Make it easier!

Discuss how Roger Hargreaves' series of *Mr Men* and *Little Miss* books personify character traits (e.g. Mr Tickle has long arms), to prompt students' imagination.

Make it harder!

Look at examples of Dickens' character descriptions from a variety of texts.

4:6 What's in a name?

1. Charles Dickens is famous for choosing particularly apt names for his characters. Often the sound of the names gives clues about the characters' personalities and traits. Review the list of character names below and pick three that appeal to you. Write a sentence explaining what impression the name gives you of the character.

   Mrs Gamp . . . .

   Mr Pecksniff. . . . .

   Mr Pinch. . . . .

   Wackford Squeers . . . .

   Magwitch . . . .

   Fagin . . . .

2. Charles Dickens' characters are often seen as being stereotypes or caricatures, in that they represent particular traits such as jealousy or charity, similar to Roger Hargreaves' *Mr Men* and *Little Miss* characters.

   You are now going to create your own caricature based on one of the following abstract nouns:

   * hope

   * anger

   * fear

   * kindness

   * greed

   Select one of the nouns and then sketch the character on a separate sheet of paper, using the prompts below to help you.

3. Once you have drawn your character to get a sense of their appearance, write a paragraph in the box below describing their personality and behaviour.

   * What does your character look like?

   * What is he/she wearing?

   * What is his/her facial expression like?

   * What is his/her body language like?

   * What is he/she holding?

   * What is he/she doing?

Ebenezer Scrooge

Introduction

In this lesson, students are introduced to Dickens' infamous character, Ebenezer Scrooge. After revising the features of imagery, students analyse the various linguistic methods that Dickens uses to describe Scrooge in Stave 1. They then produce acrostic poems to consolidate their understanding of this character.

Aims and objectives

- Extract the main points and relevant information from a text or source using a range of strategies such as skimming and scanning.
- Identify and understand the main ideas, viewpoints, themes and purposes in a text.

Starter (10 minutes)

Introduce the sentence: 'Hard and sharp as flint, from which no steel had ever struck out generous fire; secret, and self-contained, and solitary as an oyster.' Ask students to guess who is being described. Identify the examples of imagery being used and model analysis of the similes used. Comparing Scrooge to flint makes him sound as if he is devoid of human emotion; comparing him to an oyster emphasizes how isolated he makes himself from others.

Main phase (40 minutes)

- Introduce the learning objectives and lesson outcomes: to analyse the language that Dickens uses to introduce Scrooge and to create an acrostic to consolidate their knowledge of his character.
- Students read the extract from Stave 1 of *A Christmas Carol* and highlight key phrases that illuminate Scrooge's character, for example references to him being cold and others keeping their distance from him. (Explain that Dickens divided this story into staves as opposed to chapters.)
- They then write a paragraph of analysis, explaining what kind of impression the reader gets of Ebenezer Scrooge, using supporting quotes from the text.

Plenary (10 minutes)

Students create an acrostic on the task sheet using words containing the letters in Scrooge's name, e.g.:

Selfish

Cold-hearted

Homework Ideas

Ask students to illustrate their acrostics with accompanying images.

Make it easier!

Use a thesaurus to find alternative synonyms to use for the acrostic task.

Make it harder!

Ask students to write a conventional poem, rather than an acrostic, to describe Scrooge.

4:7 Ebenezer Scrooge

1. Read the following extract from stave one of Dickens' *A Christmas Carol*. Highlight words and phrases used to describe Ebenezer Scrooge that help to introduce his character.

Oh! But he was a tight-fisted hand at the grindstone, Scrooge! a squeezing, wrenching, grasping, scraping, clutching, covetous old sinner! Hard and sharp as flint, from which no steel had ever struck out generous fire; secret, and self-contained, and solitary as an oyster. The cold within him froze his old features, nipped his pointed nose, shrivelled his cheek, stiffened his gait; made his eyes red, his thin lips blue; and spoke out shrewdly in his grating voice. A frosty rime was on his head, and on his eyebrows, and his wiry chin. He carried his own low temperature always about with him; he iced his office in the dog-days; and didn't thaw it one degree at Christmas.

External heat and cold had little influence on Scrooge. No warmth could warm, no wintry weather chill him. No wind that blew was bitterer than he, no falling snow was more intent upon its purpose, no pelting rain less open to entreaty. Foul weather didn't know where to have him. The heaviest rain, and snow, and hail, and sleet, could boast of the advantage over him in only one respect. They often came down handsomely, and Scrooge never did.

Nobody ever stopped him in the street to say, with gladsome looks, 'My dear Scrooge, how are you. When will you come to see me.' No beggars implored him to bestow a trifle, no children asked him what it was o'clock, no man or woman ever once in all his life inquired the way to such and such a place, of Scrooge. Even the blind men's dogs appeared to know him; and when they saw him coming on, would tug their owners into doorways and up courts; and then would wag their tails as though they said, 'No eye at all is better than an evil eye, dark master!'

But what did Scrooge care! It was the very thing he liked. To edge his way along the crowded paths of life, warning all human sympathy to keep its distance, was what the knowing ones call 'nuts' to Scrooge.

Taken from Charles Dickens' *A Christmas Carol*

2. Now write a paragraph of analysis explaining Dickens' use of language to give the reader an impression of Scrooge's character. Don't forget to explain selected quotations from the text in detail.

3. Create an acrostic poem (see format below) using words that relate to Scrooge's character and contain letters from his name.

E . . . .   S . . . .

B . . . .   C . . . .

E . . . .   R . . . .

N . . . .   O . . . .

E . . . .   O . . . .

Z . . . .   G . . . .

E . . . .   E . . . .

R . . . .

© Helena Ceranic, 2011. *Resources for Teaching English: 11–14.*

Bah humbug!

Introduction

In this lesson, students start off by discussing various charities and their relative merits. They then read the episode from *A Christmas Carol* in which Scrooge aggressively refuses to part with any money for charitable purposes. Students then take on the role of the charity workers, discussing Scrooge's miserly behaviour.

Aims and objectives

- Explore ideas, texts and issues through a variety of dramatic approaches and conventions.
- Work on their own and with others to develop dramatic processes, narratives, performances or roles.

Starter (10 minutes)

In groups, students discuss the list of charities on the task sheet and decide which one they would choose to give money to, with reasons. Share rationale and reasoning behind each group's decisions and discuss what motivates people to give money to charity.

Main phase (35 minutes)

- Introduce the learning objectives and lesson outcomes: to explore Scrooge's attitude to charity in *A Christmas Carol* in role as charity workers from the text.
- Read the extract from *A Christmas Carol*, pausing to discuss Scrooge's argument and how the charity workers try to persuade him to change his attitude. Students then highlight key quotes that demonstrate Scrooge's mean manner.
- In pairs, students adopt the role of the two charity workers discussing their encounter with Ebenezer Scrooge; they script the dialogue between these two characters.

Plenary (15 minutes)

Listen to the charity worker dialogues and compare how groups have reflected on this episode from the text.

Homework ideas

Ask students to research an alternative charity and write a persuasive advert, convincing readers to support their worthy cause.

Make it easier!

Watch an extract on YouTube from *The Muppet Christmas Carol*, or an alternative film version of the text, to see a depiction of Scrooge's mean and aggressive response to the charity workers.

Make it harder!

Create an improvised role-play to perform in front of the class.

4:8 Bah humbug!

1. Look at the list of charities below and discuss which ones you consider to be the most worthy and why. Who would you choose to give your money to? Pick one and explain with reasons.

   Help the Aged   **RSPCA**   **Marie Curie**   **NSPCC**   **Oxfam**

2. Read the extract from *A Christmas Carol* below in which Scrooge refuses to make a donation to charity. Highlight key quotations that exhibit Scrooge's mean character.

   'At this festive season of the year, Mr Scrooge,' said the gentleman, taking up a pen, 'it is more than usually desirable that we should make some slight provision for the Poor and destitute, who suffer greatly at the present time. Many thousands are in want of common necessaries; hundreds of thousands are in want of common comforts, sir.'

   'Are there no prisons?' asked Scrooge.

   'Plenty of prisons,' said the gentleman, laying down the pen again.

   'And the Union workhouses?' demanded Scrooge. 'Are they still in operation?'

   'They are. Still,' returned the gentleman, 'I wish I could say they were not.'

   'The Treadmill and the Poor Law are in full vigour, then?' said Scrooge.

   'Both very busy, sir.'

   'Oh! I was afraid, from what you said at first, that something had occurred to stop them in their useful course,' said Scrooge. 'I'm very glad to hear it.'

   'Under the impression that they scarcely furnish Christian cheer of mind or body to the multitude,' returned the gentleman, 'a few of us are endeavouring to raise a fund to buy the Poor some meat and drink, and means of warmth. We choose this time, because it is a time, of all others, when Want is keenly felt, and Abundance rejoices. What shall I put you down for?'

   'Nothing!' Scrooge replied.

   'You wish to be anonymous?'

   'I wish to be left alone,' said Scrooge. 'Since you ask me what I wish, gentlemen, that is my answer. I don't make merry myself at Christmas and I can't afford to make idle people merry. I help to support the establishments I have mentioned: they cost enough: and those who are badly off must go there.'

   'Many can't go there; and many would rather die.'

   'If they would rather die,'' said Scrooge, 'they had better do it, and decrease the surplus population. Besides – excuse me – I don't know that.'

   'But you might know it,' observed the gentleman.

   'It's not my business,' Scrooge returned. 'It's enough for a man to understand his own business, and not to interfere with other people's. Mine occupies me constantly. Good afternoon, gentlemen!'

Taken from Charles Dickens' *A Christmas Carol.*

3. In character as the two charity workers, create a role-play dialogue discussing what has just happened. In your script, include your reflections on Scrooge's attitude towards helping others.

Christmas priorities

Introduction

In this lesson, students debate the true meaning of Christmas. They start by prioritising different activities that are traditionally associated with Christmas Day. Students then prepare for a debate in which they argue in role for or against a specific proposal. Students will be assessed on their ability to discuss effectively and convincingly in character.

Aims and objectives

- Help discussions succeed by acknowledging and responding to the contributions of others.
- Take different roles in group discussion as required by the task or context.

Starter (15 minutes)

Students look at the list of Christmas priorities and see whether they agree with the order of importance they have been sorted into. They then discuss their views in groups and decide on their own order of priority. They can replicate the priority diamond in their own books and compare with the original during feedback.

Main phase (40 minutes)

- Introduce the learning objectives and lesson outcomes: to argue successfully in role during a Christmas debate. Discuss the debate options on the task sheet and look at the exemplar plan. Designate debate topics to groups.
- Students plan ideas for their chosen debates and agree on roles and perspectives; which characters will group members adopt and what perspective will they be arguing for?
- Once students have had a chance to prepare in role and agree on the format of their debate, set up the classroom appropriately and start to observe the debate performances. The scenario can be a council meeting, with the audience treated as community members.

Plenary (5 minutes)

Review the debates and identify particularly authentic and impressive performances, with reasons.

Homework ideas

Ask students to research the Keep Sunday Special website (www.keepsundayspecial.org.uk) and write a paragraph explaining their opinions on this campaign.

Make it easier!

Provide students with starter sentences to help them to contribute to the debate, e.g. 'With respect . . .'; 'Although I understand why you might think that . . .'; 'That's fair enough, but . . .'

Make it harder!

Treat the task as a Socratic discussion where the audience members around the edge of the debate observe for particular features. More information about this style of speaking and listening activity can be found on the English Secondary National Strategy website:

http://nationalstrategies.standards.dcsf.gov.uk/node/85876/

4:9 Christmas priorities

1. Look at the list of Christmas activities below and decide on an order of priority; which ones do you think are most important? Which are least important? Discuss your opinions in your groups and create your own priority diamond, with the most important Christmas activity at the top of the diamond. You may need to compromise to reach a common decision.

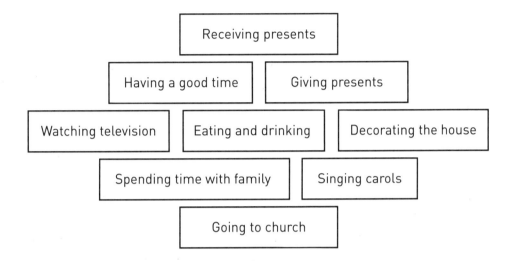

2. In groups, prepare for one of the following Christmas debates. Decide who will be for and against the proposal and delegate specific roles and arguments to members of the group. Look at the first example for ideas, then prepare arguments and ideas in role in note form in the box provided.

Everyone should have Christmas dinner at a restaurant

For: **Mum** (can enjoy the day properly – she won't have to spend it slaving in the kitchen)

    Restaurant manager (everyone can have a decent meal without the stress and hassle)

Against: **Waitress** (wants a day off on Christmas to spend with her own family)

    Local grocer (Christmas is traditionally a time to enjoy cooking for your family)

Debate options:

- Everyone should invite a lonely or homeless person to Christmas dinner.

- Everyone should go to church on Christmas Day.

- Presents should be banned and money given to charity instead.

- Shops should be open on Christmas Day.

Debate: . . . .

For:

Against:

Do you believe in ghosts?

Introduction

In this lesson, students discuss their own assumptions and opinions about ghosts before examining Scrooge's encounters with the ghosts of Christmas past, present and future in *A Christmas Carol*. They analyse the effects that the ghosts have on Scrooge's character and consider how and why Scrooge's attitude changes throughout the course of the story.

Aims and objectives

- Make a personal response to a text and provide some textual reference in support.
- Understand the different ways texts can reflect the social, cultural and historical contexts in which they were written.

Starter (10 minutes)

Ask students to explore their beliefs surrounding the topic of ghosts using the prompts on the task sheet. Feed back and share students' opinions and experiences on this subject matter.

Main phase (40 minutes)

- Introduce the learning objectives and lesson outcomes: to explore how ghosts are presented in Dickens' *A Christmas Carol* and examine how Scrooge's character is affected by them.
- Students read the two extracts from the text which focus on Scrooge's first and last encounter with a ghost in the story. They discuss Scrooge's reactions and highlight key quotations.
- They then write a paragraph explaining how the ghosts affect Scrooge, using supporting details from the text.

Plenary (10 minutes)

Ask students to consider the significance and importance of the ghosts in Dickens' *A Christmas Carol* and discuss whether social attitudes towards ghosts have changed much since the text was written.

Homework ideas

Ask students to research Victorian beliefs about ghosts and the supernatural and make notes about this.

Make it easier!

Model quote analysis with the class: select a quote that reveals Scrooge's reaction to one of the ghosts and then explain what effect Dickens' choice of language has on the reader.

Make it harder!

Ask students to consider how Scrooge's level of fear and interest towards the ghosts changes as the story progresses, and why.

4:10 Do you believe in ghosts?

1. Think of all of the films or television programmes that that you have seen that contain ghosts, e.g. *Ghostbusters*, *The Others*, or *Casper the Friendly Ghost*. Discuss the questions below:

   - Do you find ghost films scary?

   - Do you believe in ghosts?

2. In *A Christmas Carol*, Ebenezer Scrooge encounters four different ghosts. Read the extracts taken from the first and last encounters below and analyse the kinds of effects that the ghosts' presence and words have on Scrooge. Which one does he find most scary and why?

Jacob Marley's Ghost

'You don't believe in me,' observed the Ghost.

   'I don't,' said Scrooge.

   'What evidence would you have of my reality beyond that of your senses?'

   'I don't know,' said Scrooge.

   'Why do you doubt your senses?'

   'Because,' said Scrooge, 'a little thing affects them. A slight disorder of the stomach makes them cheats. You may be an undigested bit of beef, a blot of mustard, a crumb of cheese, a fragment of an underdone potato. There's more of gravy than grave about you, whatever you are.'

The Ghost of Christmas Future

Although well used to ghostly company by this time, Scrooge feared the silent shape so much that his legs trembled beneath him, and he found that he could hardly stand when he prepared to follow it. The Spirit paused a moment, as observing his condition, and giving him time to recover.

   But Scrooge was all the worse for this. It thrilled him with a vague uncertain horror, to know that behind the dusky shroud, there were ghostly eyes intently fixed upon him, while he, though he stretched his own to the utmost, could see nothing but a spectral hand and one great heap of black.

   'Ghost of the Future!' he exclaimed, 'I fear you more than any spectre I have seen. But as I know your purpose is to do me good, and as I hope to live to be another man from what I was, I am prepared to bear you company, and do it with a thankful heart. Will you not speak to me?'

   It gave him no reply. The hand was pointed straight before them.

   'Lead on!' said Scrooge. 'Lead on! The night is waning fast, and it is precious time to me, I know. Lead on, Spirit!'

Taken from Charles Dickens' *A Christmas Carol*.

Introduction

In this lesson, students consider how and why Scrooge's character has dramatically changed throughout the course of *A Christmas Carol*. After comparing quotations from the start and the end of the story, students take on the guise of Scrooge's life coach in order to catalogue and report the changes that they have noticed.

Aims and objectives

- Draw on the conventions of written forms to plan writing and develop ideas to fit a specific task.
- Make improvements to a piece of writing as it progresses by developing techniques for editing, proofreading and making revisions.

Starter (10 minutes)

Ask students to read the various quotations on the task sheet and sort them into two categories according to whether they were taken from the first or last stave of the story. Feed back and discuss the way in which the quotes show how Scrooge's personality has changed.

Main phase (40 minutes)

- Introduce the learning objectives and lesson outcomes: to write a report, in the role of Scrooge's life coach, about the changes to his character that have happened throughout the text. Ensure that students understand the role of a life coach.
- Ask students to discuss the way in which the quotes demonstrate how Scrooge has changed from a cold, mean and miserly man to an open, giving and happy one – focus on Dickens' use of language.
- Students use their prior knowledge of the text to write their life coach case study report. Ask them to fill in the details at the bottom of the task sheet and then write the report on a separate piece of paper or in their books. They can use their imagination to add to their knowledge of the text.

Plenary (10 minutes)

Peer-assess the life coach reports and identify areas for editing and revising. Students add further explanation or modify language used according to feedback.

Homework ideas

Ask students to create an alternative list of the Ten Commandments from the Bible, relevant to Scrooge's character, e.g. *Thou shalt not be mean with thy money.*

Make it easier!

Discuss content ideas for the life coach report and create a writing frame with the class.

Make it harder!

Ask students to include quotes from the starter activity in their life coach reports.

4:11 Scrooge's life coach

1. Look at the list of quotations about Scrooge below, cut them up and sort them into two piles, depending on whether they have been taken from the beginning or the end of *A Christmas Carol*. Consider what kind of person Scrooge is depicted as, to help you to decide.

> He had been sobbing violently in his conflict with the Spirit, and his face was wet with tears.

> 'I am as light as a feather, I am as happy as an angel, I am as merry as a schoolboy.'

> A squeezing, wrenching, grasping, scraping, clutching, covetous, old sinner!

> But he was a tight-fisted hand at the grind- stone, Scrooge!

> Hard and sharp as flint, from which no steel had ever struck out generous fire.

> Secret, and self-contained, and solitary as an oyster.

> 'I don't know what to do!' cried Scrooge, laughing and crying in the same breath.

> He was so fluttered and so glowing with his good intentions, that his broken voice would scarcely answer to his call.

2. Now, using the quotations to help you, consider how and why Scrooge's character has dramatically changed over the course of the story. Imagine that you are Scrooge's life coach. Write a report cataloguing and explaining the changes that you have observed taking place. Use the template below to help you get started.

Life Coach Case Report

Name: . . . .

Address: . . . .

Occupation: . . . .

Date of first meeting: . . . .

No. of sessions: . . . .

Please outline the client's case history and progress on a separate sheet of paper.

Scrooge's Christmas message

Introduction

In this lesson, students familiarise themselves with the format and style of the Queen's annual Christmas message. They then write the script for Scrooge's Christmas message based on what he has learned by the end of the story and what messages he wants to share with the rest of the world.

Aims and objectives

* Identify key features of speech in a variety of contexts, and some key skills and strategies used by speakers.
* Use the main conventions of standard English when appropriate.

Starter (15 minutes)

Watch the Queen's Christmas message, available on YouTube. Ask students to note down the content, style and form of the speech: what does she speak about and what kind of language does she use? Share ideas.

Main phase (30 minutes)

* Introduce the learning objectives and lesson outcomes: to create an alternative Christmas message from Ebenezer Scrooge, using the conventions of the Queen's speech and their knowledge of Scrooge's character.
* Students reflect on stave five of *A Christmas Carol* and plan ideas for what Scrooge would choose to talk about in his Christmas message. Ask them to consider what lessons he has learned and what messages he would want to share with the rest of mankind.
* Students start to draft their speeches, ensuring that they are structured appropriately and use the Standard English that they identified in the Queen's Christmas message.

Plenary (15 minutes)

Students perform their Christmas speeches and are assessed for appropriateness of content and style.

Homework ideas

Ask students to create a newspaper article reporting the transformation in Ebenezer Scrooge.

Make it easier!

Watch the end of *Scrooged*, starring Bill Murray and available on YouTube, to get ideas for Scrooge's Christmas message.

Make it harder!

Students perform their Christmas speeches to each other and peer-evaluate.

4:12 Scrooge's Christmas message

1. Watch the Queen's Christmas message and make notes about the speech in the circles below.

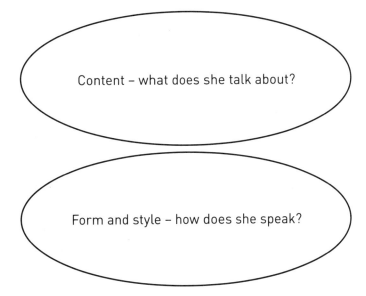

Content – what does she talk about?

Form and style – how does she speak?

2. You are now going to write an alternative Christmas speech, spoken by Ebenezer Scrooge at the end of *A Christmas Carol*. Plan the ideas for the content of Scrooge's Christmas message in the space below.

What would Scrooge include in his Christmas message?

3. Now use your ideas to write Scrooge's Christmas message. Don't forget to refer to events from the text and make sure that the style of the speech is in keeping with this genre of text.

Poetry devices

Introduction

In this lesson, students revise poetic techniques and explore the features of different genres of poetry. They then create their own haiku, following stylistic rules, based on a season of their choice.

Aims and objectives

- Explain how specific choices and combinations of form, layout and presentation create particular effects.
- Create considered and appropriate effects by drawing independently on the range and variety of their own vocabulary, and by using strategies and resources to extend their available choices.

Starter (15 minutes)

Students match up the poetry terms to their definitions on the task sheet. Discuss which ones students are most confident with and explain the more tricky ones together.

Main phase (35 minutes)

- Introduce the learning objectives and lesson outcomes: to familiarise students with poetic terms and forms and create a haiku using the poetic conventions.
- Ask students to write a definition of the three different poems listed on the task sheet (limerick, ode and haiku) using dictionaries and prior knowledge. Share findings.
- Students create their own haiku, sticking to the conventions (three lines of five, seven, five syllables, focusing on a season). If students have time, they should create a haiku for each season and decorate appropriately.

Plenary (10 minutes)

Share haikus within groups and pick the best to share with the rest of the class.

Homework ideas

Ask students to illustrate their haikus and present them for display.

Make it easier!

Read out sample haikus as a class, clapping to identify the syllable count.

Make it harder!

Source examples of famous odes to share with the class, e.g. Keats' *Ode to a Nightingale*, to exemplify this particular genre.

5.1 Poetry devices

1. Look at the definitions of poetic techniques in the grid below and match them up with the list of devices below.

A figure of speech in which one thing is compared to another, e.g. He fought like a lion in battle	When words or syllables sound the same at the endings of lines of verse	The formation of words that imitate the sounds associated with the object or action they refer to, e.g. pop and sizzle
To represent an idea in a human form or as a thing having a human characteristic, e.g. The tree shook with fear	Comparing two like objects by saying that one is the other, e.g. He is a lion in battle	The occurrence of the same letter or sound at the beginning of a group of words for effect, e.g. Sing a song of sixpence
Similarity of vowel sounds in words that do not completely rhyme, e.g. vermin and furnish	The pattern of sound produced by long, short or stressed syllables in words	A verse of poetry

Techniques

Rhyme

Onomatopoeia

Rhythm

Metaphor

Personification

Assonance

Simile

Alliteration

Stanza

2. Now use dictionaries and prior knowledge to define the conventions of the following types of poetry. Write down a list of 'rules' that each type of poetry follows.

Limerick   **Haiku**   **Ode**

3. Look at the example of a haiku below and label the common features that you have researched.

> Little daffodil
> Peeping through the softened soil
> Spring is beginning

4. Now create your own haiku and decorate appropriately. Don't forget to stick to the stylistic conventions for this genre of poetry.

Ode to an everyday object

Introduction
In this lesson, students look at a parody of an ode in order to develop their knowledge of the features of this type of poetry. They then create their own comical ode to an everyday object, using the poetic techniques that they have identified.

Aims and objectives
- Respond to a text by making precise points and providing relevant evidence in support of those points.
- Draw on some techniques and devices used by writers in order to develop distinctive character and voice in their own fiction.

Starter (10 minutes)
Recap students' prior knowledge of the poetic genre of odes (this links to lesson 5:1). Introduce the title 'Ode to a jelly tot' and share expectations of the poem's style and content. Read the poem together and discuss first impressions.

Main phase (40 minutes)
- Introduce the learning objectives and outcomes: to identify the features of a traditional ode used in the exemplar poem and write their own ode dedicated to an everyday object.
- Students underline and annotate the poetic features they can spot within the poem, including the devices in the following list (students may need help with unfamiliar terms such as hyperbole – use dictionaries if necessary).
  — second person pronouns
  — hyperbole and exclamations
  — onomatopoeia
  — sensory description
  — alliteration
  — metaphorical language
- Students choose an object to be the subject for their own ode and draft a poem using the same poetic conventions.

Plenary (10 minutes)
Students evaluate each other's poems and identify how many devices have been used.

Homework ideas
Ask students to create a poem that is the antithesis of an ode, communicating their hatred and disgust towards an everyday object.

Make it easier!
Provide students with a range of starter sentences to help them with the construction of their ode. For example: 'Oh . . . you make me feel like . . .'; 'You are the best . . .'; 'When I see you I . . .'

Make it harder!
Introduce the term 'parody' and explore how the students' poems are examples of parodies of the original poetry genre.

www.ehow.com/how_2118173_write-parody-poem.html

5:2 Ode to an everyday object

1. Read the example of an ode below; it is a playful version of this genre of poetry.

> **Ode to a Jelly Tot**
> Oh jelly tot!
> You art the most scrumptious confectionery of all.
> Your sugary crystals sizzle on my tongue
> And leave me fizzing.
> Bursting with tropical flavours,
> You transport my mouth to exotic beaches.
> Your ambrosial flavours fill my palate with joy
> And my heart with glee!
> You are my delicious diamonds of sweetness.

2. Identify and annotate the language devices that have been used in the poem, using the list below.

   - second person pronouns
   - hyperbole
   - exclamations
   - onomatopoeia
   - sensory description
   - alliteration
   - metaphorical language

3. Now select an everyday object of your choice to be the subject of your ode. Make sure that it is suitably mundane – this will help to provide humour in your ode. For example, you could write an ode to belly button fluff, kitchen scales or football socks. Draft your ode ideas in the box below.

Soundscapes

Introduction

In this lesson, students revise onomatopoeic words, their purpose and effect in poetry. In groups, they then create soundscapes based on a particular venue. This involves students collating a wide range of sounds that they associate with a specific busy location. They then use these sounds to create noisy performance poetry.

Aims and objectives

- Develop and sustain processes, narratives, performances and roles through the use of a variety of dramatic conventions, techniques and styles.
- Draw on a repertoire of linguistic and literary techniques, and select those most appropriate for creating specific effects in their own writing.

Starter (10 minutes)

Introduce the term onomatopoeia and ask students to write down as many onomatopoeic words as they can. Share lists of words and discuss the effect that onomatopoeic words have in texts. Introduce the idea that while landscape is a word that refers to the view that can be seen, soundscapes can represent the sounds that can be heard in a particular scene.

Main phase (35 minutes)

- Introduce the learning objectives and outcomes: to create a poetic soundscape that depicts a particular noisy venue and perform this to the class.
- Designate the venues on the accompanying task sheet to groups of students – do this discreetly so that the locations remain a secret (you may wish to cut up a spare copy of the task sheet and hand out the locations). Students then discuss and generate a range of sounds, including onomatopoeic words, that could be heard at their venue and write all of the noises down on A3 paper.
- Students prepare to present their soundscapes to the class by deciding on the noises that each of them will perform – they should create a montage of sounds, with noises overlapping, so that the audience can get a good sense of the atmosphere of the location.

Plenary (15 minutes)

Perform the soundscapes and guess locations based on the noises that students perform.

Homework ideas

Ask students to write a poem about their favourite place – remind them to include atmospheric sounds.

Make it easier!

Provide students with pictures of the locations to stimulate their imagination or model an example together.

Make it harder!

Introduce the term sibilance (the repetition of the 's' sound) and encourage students to use this technique in their soundscapes.

5:3 Soundscapes

1. Think of as many onomatopoeic words as you can and list them below. Three examples are given to start you off.

Snap   Crackle   Pop

2. Why do writers use onomatopoeia in their texts? Explain the effect of this particular device in the space below.

   . . . .

   . . . .

3. You will be given one of the following noisy locations in your groups in order to create a soundscape. Make a list of all of the sounds and noises you would expect to hear at that venue – remember to include onomatopoeic words.

Swimming pool	Football stadium
Airport lounge	Supermarket checkout
Busy restaurant	Industrial kitchen
Market	A&E ward

4. You now need to prepare to perform your soundscape to the rest of the class. Consider how you will divide the noises up among your group and how you will recreate the atmosphere of your scene by using a wide range of rich sounds and noises.

Love poetry

Introduction

In this lesson, students explore the meanings of the words realist, cynic and romantic before considering the clichéd features of romantic poetry. Students are introduced to the conventions of a Shakespearian sonnet before looking at 'Sonnet 18' in detail.

Aims and objectives

- Explore the concept of literary heritage, why certain texts are important within it and how some texts have influenced culture and thinking.
- Explain how specific structural and organizational choices in texts create particular effects.

Starter (10 minutes)

Define the terms realist, cynic and romantic using dictionaries. Discuss how 'romantic' can mean different things in different contexts. Share students' assumptions about love poetry – what kind of romantic sentiments do they expect it to contain?

Main phase (40 minutes)

- Introduce the learning objectives and lesson outcomes: to understand the features of a Shakespearian sonnet and be able to explain what kinds of themes and relationships this form of poetry presents.
- Read Shakespeare's 'Sonnet 18' together, pausing to discuss difficult vocabulary and phrasing. Ask students to identify what they notice about the poem's structure, style and content by looking for the following features:
  — syllable count
  — poem's subject matter
  — number of lines
  — rhyme scheme
- Feed back students' findings and ask students to make notes about the features of a sonnet, with supporting examples.

Plenary (10 minutes)

Consider what kind of relationship is portrayed in the sonnet. Who has the upper hand; who has control of the relationship? How are women viewed in this period of time? Students write down their reflections.

Homework ideas

Ask students to find and read three more sonnets written by Shakespeare and write down their views of them.

Make it easier!

Support students by modelling annotation to identify poetic features.

Make it harder!

Ask students to identify and comment on Shakespeare's use of nature imagery as well.

5:4 Love poetry

1. Use a dictionary to find definitions for the following terms:

   Realist: . . . .

   Cynic: . . . .

   Romantic: . . . .

2. What do you consider to be the features of love poetry? Make notes around the heart shape below.

3. Sonnets were very popular forms of love poetry during the sixteenth century. Shakespeare wrote over a hundred sonnets in his career; 'Sonnet 18' is one of his most famous. Look for the following features in the sonnet. Annotate the poem to identify the poetic techniques used (see list below).

   - syllable count (the number of beats per line)

   - poem's subject matter (what/who is it about?)

   - number of lines (how many lines long is the whole poem?)

   - rhyme scheme (look at the last word of every line – what pattern do you notice?)

   Sonnet 18

   Shall I compare thee to a summer's day?

   Thou art more lovely and more temperate:

   Rough winds do shake the darling buds of May,

   And summer's lease hath all too short a date:

   Sometime too hot the eye of heaven shines,

   And often is his gold complexion dimm'd;

   And every fair from fair sometime declines,

   By chance or nature's changing course untrimmed;

   But thy eternal summer shall not fade

   Nor lose possession of that fair thou owest;

   Nor shall Death brag thou wander'st in his shade,

   When in eternal lines to time thou growest:

   So long as men can breathe or eyes can see,

   So long lives this and this gives life to thee.

© Helena Ceranic, 2011. *Resources for Teaching English: 11–14.*

Shakespeare's sonnets

Resources
Copies of 'Sonnet 18' from lesson 5:4

Introduction

In this lesson, students develop their study of Shakespearean sonnets as a continuation of lesson 5:4. They sort extracts from 'Sonnet 130', using their knowledge of the structural conventions of this genre of poetry. They then compare the content and style of this sonnet with the more conventional 'Sonnet 18'.

Aims and objectives

- Make relevant notes when researching different sources, comparing and contrasting information.
- Broaden their experience of reading a wide range of texts and express their preferences and opinions.

Starter (15 minutes)

Recap the conventions of a Shakespeare sonnet, learned in lesson 5:4, and then ask students to attempt to put the extracts from 'Sonnet 130' on the task sheet in the correct order. Give feedback on students' attempts to put the sonnet's extracts in order.

Main phase (35 minutes)

- Introduce the learning objectives and lesson outcomes: to consolidate understanding of the conventions of a Shakespearean sonnet and compare two sonnets to consider how Shakespeare used this genre of poetry.
- Discuss students' first impressions of 'Sonnet 130'. What do they notice is similar to or different from 'Sonnet 18'?
- In pairs, students read both sonnets again in detail and complete the questions on the task sheet.

Plenary (10 minutes)

Share responses and discuss which sonnet students prefer and why.

Homework ideas

Ask students to research Shakespeare's marriage and love life to inform their reading of the sonnets. They should write a paragraph summarising what they have found out.

Make it easier!

Complete comprehension questions together with students.

Make it harder!

Ask students to write their own sonnets, either in the vein of 'Sonnet 18' or 'Sonnet 130', using the conventions that they have identified and learned about.

5:5 Shakespeare's sonnets

1. Use your knowledge of the structural 'rules' of Shakespearean sonnets to try to put the extracts from this sonnet ('Sonnet 130') in the correct order. The first two lines are accurate.

Sonnet 130

 1. My mistress' eyes are nothing like the sun;
 2. Coral is far more red than her lips' red.
 3. ....
 4. ....
 5. ....
 6. ....
 7. ....
 8. ....
 9. ....
10. ....
11. ....
12. ....
13. ....
14. ....

> And in some perfumes is there more delight
> Than in the breath that from my mistress reeks.
>
> And yet, by heaven, I think my love as rare
> As any she belied with false compare.
>
> I love to hear her speak, yet well I know
> That music hath a far more pleasing sound.
>
> I have seen roses damasked, red and white,
> But no such roses see I in her cheeks;
>
> If snow be white, why then her breasts are dun;
> If hairs be wires, black wires grow on her head.
>
> I grant I never saw a goddess go:
> My mistress, when she walks, treads on the ground.

2. Now compare the content and style of 'Sonnet 130' with 'Sonnet 18' by answering the following questions.

   1. What is conventional about 'Sonnet 130's':

      a) subject matter?

      ....

      b) language and structure?

      ....

   2. How does this sonnet differ from 'Sonnet 18'?

      ....

   3. Why do you think Shakespeare wrote this sonnet?

      ....

Imagery activities

Introduction

In this lesson, students revise imagery techniques and practise developing their own metaphorical comparisons. They then read 'The Thickness of Ice', a poem by Liz Loxley, which uses an extended metaphor, comparing the development of a romantic relationship to skaters on the ice. Students then analyse the effect that the imagery has on the reader.

Aims and objectives

- Use inference and deduction to explore layers of meaning within a text.
- Explain how linguistic concepts are related, and use the terminology in ways that help them describe and review language use.

Starter (10 minutes)

Recap the term 'imagery' and the linguistic devices that are included within this term.

www.poetryarchive.org/poetryarchive/glossaryItem.do?id=8098

Students make notes on the task sheet.

Main phase (40 minutes)

- Introduce the learning objectives and lesson outcomes: to familiarise students with the use and effect of metaphors.
- Students create their own metaphorical comparisons by choosing objects that represent people they know well and explaining the links.
- Students then read the poem by Liz Loxley and identify lines that exemplify the poet's use of an extended metaphor.

Plenary (10 minutes)

Students write an analytical paragraph, using their identified quotes, explaining the effect of the imagery in the poem and using the prompts provided on the task sheet.

Homework ideas

Ask students to identify song lyrics that contain imagery and write a paragraph explaining how imagery is used by the artist.

Make it easier!

Model writing the analytical paragraph with the students.

Make it harder!

Ask students to write their own poems, in the style of 'The Thickness of Ice', using a central metaphor. They may choose to compare a developing friendship to a game of tennis, for example.

5:6 Imagery activities

1. Use a dictionary and prior knowledge to define the term 'imagery' and think of a range of linguistic techniques that are used within imagery. Write your ideas in the box below.

> Imagery:

2. Choose a person you know really well – it could be a relative or best friend. Follow the prompts below to create metaphorical comparisons.

   - Imagine your chosen person was an item of furniture. What would they be and why? *E.g. Chaise longue because they are laid back and sophisticated.*

   - Now imagine your chosen person was an item of food. What would they be and why? *E.g. Chocolate cup cake because they are cute, naughty but nice.*

   - What would they be if they were an item of clothing? *E.g. Wooly scarf because they are soft and comforting.*

3. Read the poem below by Liz Loxley in which she uses imagery to describe a relationship.

   The Thickness of Ice

   At first we will meet as friends
   (Though secretly I'll be hoping
   We'll become much more
   And hoping that you're hoping that too).

   At first we'll be like skaters
   Testing the thickness of ice
   (With each meeting
   We'll skate nearer the centre of the lake).

   Later we will become less anxious to impress,
   Less eager than the skater going for gold,
   (The triple jumps and spins
   Will become an old routine:
   We will be content with simple movements).

   Later we will not notice the steady thaw,
   The creeping cracks will be ignored,
   (And one day when the ice gives way
   We will scramble to save ourselves
   And not each other).

   Last of all we'll meet as acquaintances
   (Though secretly we'll be enemies,
   Hurt by missing out on a medal,
   Jealous of new partners).

   Last of all we'll be like children
   Having learnt the thinness of ice,
   (Though secretly, perhaps, we may be hoping
   To break the ice between us
   And maybe meet again as friends).

4. Identify metaphorical quotes in the poem – lines that suggest that Liz is referring to more than just ice skating.

5. Now write a paragraph explaining how the poet has used imagery effectively.

   - How is she comparing a developing relationship to the experience of two ice skaters?

   - What message does the poem give about the relationship between two people?

Ageing poems

Introduction

In this lesson, students explore Shakespeare's 'Seven Ages of Man' and identify the different stages as depicted in the text. Once they have looked at Shakespeare's metaphorical presentation of life, they will create their own modernised versions in groups and perform to the rest of the class.

Aims and objectives

- Trace the development of a writer's ideas, viewpoint and themes.
- Use specific dramatic approaches and conventions in structured ways for effective exploration of ideas, texts, issues and themes.

Starter (5 minutes)

Introduce the title 'The Seven Ages of Man'. Ask students to generate names for the seven stages of human life, e.g. babies, toddlers, teenagers. Compare students' ideas.

Main phase (40 minutes)

- Introduce the learning objectives and lesson outcomes: to explore Shakespeare's text 'The Seven Ages of Man' and produce a modernised version.
- Read the text together, discussing the difficult words and the meaning of the poem.
- Students highlight the seven stages mentioned in the text and draw images in the corresponding boxes to denote the ages described by Shakespeare.
- In their groups they then devise their own versions of the text, using modernised language and variations in the stages.

Plenary (15 minutes)

Students perform their new versions of 'The Seven Ages of Man' and evaluate each other's creative ideas.

Homework ideas

Ask students to create a poem about the seven stages of another topic, e.g. a football match; a trip to the hairdressers.

Make it easier!

Model how to modernise the content and language of the text by completing an example together, e.g. 'The first stage of life is when a baby is born, crying and being sick . . .'

Make it harder!

Ask students to focus on Shakespeare's use of an extended metaphor to present human life as if it were a series of performances on stage and discuss the effect of his use of imagery and what it suggests about the life cycle.

5:7 Ageing poems

1. If you had to divide human life into seven different stages, what would they be? List your ideas below.

   1. . . . .   2. . . . .   3. . . . .

   4. . . . .   5. . . . .   6. . . . .

   7. . . . .

2. Read the extract below from Shakespeare's play *As You Like It*. It uses an extended metaphor to compare human life to a performance on stage by actors.

3. Identify the seven stages of life that Shakespeare refers to and draw a line to the seven boxes on the right-hand side. Then draw a picture in each box to symbolise man at each stage of his life.

   'The Seven Ages of Man'

   All the world's a stage,
   And all the men and women merely players,
   They have their exits and entrances,
   And one man in his time plays many parts,
   His acts being seven ages. At first the infant,
   Mewling and puking in the nurse's arms.
   Then, the whining schoolboy with his satchel
   And shining morning face, creeping like snail
   Unwillingly to school. And then the lover,
   Sighing like furnace, with a woeful ballad
   Made to his mistress' eyebrow. Then a soldier,
   Full of strange oaths, and bearded like the pard,
   Jealous in honour, sudden, and quick in quarrel,
   Seeking the bubble reputation
   Even in the cannon's mouth. And then the justice
   In fair round belly, with good capon lined,
   With eyes severe, and beard of formal cut,
   Full of wise saws, and modern instances,
   And so he plays his part.
   The sixth age shifts
   Into the lean and slippered pantaloon,
   With spectacles on nose, and pouch on side,
   His youthful hose well saved, a world too wide,
   For his shrunk shank, and his big manly voice,
   Turning again towards childish treble, pipes
   And whistles in his sound. Last scene of all,
   That ends this strange eventful history,
   Is second childishness and mere oblivion,
   Sans teeth, sans eyes, sans taste, sans everything.

4. Now create your own modernised version of the seven ages of man. Consider what seven stages you would pick and how you would describe them.

War poetry bias

Introduction

In this lesson, students recap the concept of bias before generating adjectives that give contrasting views of war. Students then read 'Fall In', a poem written by Harold Begbie during the First World War, and analyse the techniques used to persuade young men to enlist. They then compare the title of this poem to others written in the same period to consider how bias is evident.

Aims and objectives

- Use a range of reading strategies to retrieve relevant information and main points from texts, distinguishing between fact and opinion where appropriate.
- Respond to a text by making precise points and providing relevant evidence in support of those points.

Starter (15 minutes)

Discuss the term 'bias' with the students and check their prior knowledge, with examples. Ask students to define bias on the task sheet (a preference or an inclination, especially one that inhibits impartial judgement) and fill in the war grid with positive and negative adjectives. Share and discuss ideas.

Main phase (30 minutes)

- Introduce the learning objectives and lesson outcomes: to analyse a poem written during the First World War and explore the reasons behind the poet's messages about war.
- Read 'Fall In' by Harold Begbie and annotate the persuasive techniques used in the poem to convince men to enlist (emotional blackmail, repetition, contrasting pairs).
- Discuss how and why this poem would have successfully roused the young men of England (made them feel guilty, obliged, unpopular if they didn't take part).

Plenary (15 minutes)

Ask students to write a paragraph explaining the motivations behind the poem 'Fall In', using quotations to support their views. Share and discuss.

Homework ideas

Ask students to use the internet to explore Harold Begbie's biography and write a paragraph explaining how and why his opinions on war changed during his lifetime.

Make it easier!

Complete the annotation activity together with the class.

Make it harder!

Focus on the title of the poem 'Fall In' and introduce two other poem titles 'Who's for the Game?' by Jessie Pope and 'Dulce et Decorum Est Pro Patria Mori' (It is sweet and fitting to die for one's country) by Wilfred Owen. Explain what the titles mean and discuss how they give a positive spin on the war effort, with the exception of Owen who is using sarcasm in his (in the poem he refers to the title as 'that old lie').

5:8 War poetry bias

1. Define the term 'bias' and give an example below.

   Bias: ....

   ....

2. Complete the grid below with contrasting adjectives to describe war and fighting. A few examples are included.

Positive	Negative
heroic courageous	bloody barbaric

3. Now read the First World War poem by Harold Begbie, 'Fall In'. Consider what kind of impression this poem gives about joining the war effort.

   Fall In

   What will you lack, sonny, what will you lack,
   When the girls line up the street
   Shouting their love to the lads to come back
   From the foe they rushed to beat?
   Will you send a strangled cheer to the sky
   And grin till your cheeks are red?
   But what will you lack when your mate
     goes by
   With a girl who cuts you dead?

   Where will you look, sonny, where will
     you look,
   When your children yet to be
   Clamour to learn of the part you took
   In the War that kept men free?
   Will you say it was naught to you if France
   Stood up to her foe or bunked?
   But where will you look when they give
     the glance
   That tells you they know you funked?

   How will you fare, sonny, how will you fare
   In the far-off winter night,
   When you sit by the fire in an old man's chair
   And your neighbours talk of the fight?
   Will you slink away, as it were from a blow,
   Your old head shamed and bent?
   Or say – I was not with the first to go,
   But I went, thank God, I went?

   Why do they call, sonny, why do they call
   For men who are brave and strong?
   Is it naught to you if your country fall,
   And Right is smashed by Wrong?
   Is it football still and the picture show,
   The pub and the betting odds,
   When your brothers stand to the tyrant's
     blow,
   And England's call is God's!

4. Why do you think Harold Begbie wrote this poem? What were his motivations? Explain the effect the language would have had on the poet's target audience, using supporting quotations from the text.

The Lady of Shalott

Introduction

In this lesson, students are introduced to the mysterious figure from the Alfred Lord Tennyson ballad. They review newspaper headlines including clues about the poem to predict the text's events. They then read part one of the narrative poem and draw and label a picture of the tapestry woven by the Lady in the poem to familiarise themselves with the poem's setting.

Aims and objectives

- Broaden their experience of reading a wide range of texts and express their preferences and opinions.
- Experiment with different ways of presenting texts, drawing on a range of modes, formats and media with the needs of the reader in mind.

Starter (10 minutes)

Students read the newspaper-style headlines based on the poem 'The Lady of Shalott' and predict events from the clues in the title. Share ideas and guesses.

Main phase (45 minutes)

- Introduce the learning objectives and lesson outcomes: to explore the poem's character, setting and events, and produce a picture of the Lady of Shalott's tapestry, based on evidence from the text.
- Students read parts one and two of the poem, pausing to discuss key information and to identify the poem's form and structure.
- After sharing observations with the class, students identify scenery, people and objects that would feature in the Lady's tapestry, based on the descriptions in the poem.
- Students create their own tapestry pictures.

Plenary (5 minutes)

Peer-evaluate tapestries and check contents against the poem.

Homework ideas

Ask students to research Arthurian legend and find out and make notes about how the Lady of Shalott featured in it.

Make it easier!

Explain the conventions of a ballad before introducing the poem.

www.answers.com/topic/ballad/

Make it harder!

Ask students to label their tapestry with accompanying quotations from the poem.

5:9 The Lady of Shalott

1. Look at the newspaper headlines below. Discuss what events they may be refering to and predict what you think that this poem may be about.

Curse shrouds island

Lady is half sick of shadows

Mysterious death shocks Camelot

2. Alfred Lord Tennyson's 'The Lady of Shalott' is a narrative poem – a poem that tells a story. It has four parts in total. Read parts one and two below. Then on a separate piece of paper or in your books draw a picture of the tapestry that she weaves, including the people and scenery. Label the items with quotations from the poem.

The Lady of Shalott

Part I

On either side the river lie
Long fields of barley and of rye,
That clothe the wold and meet the sky;
And thro' the field the road runs by
To many-tower'd Camelot;
And up and down the people go,
Gazing where the lilies blow
Round an island there below,
The island of Shalott.

Willows whiten, aspens quiver,
Little breezes dusk and shiver
Thro' the wave that runs for ever
By the island in the river
Flowing down to Camelot.
Four gray walls, and four gray towers,
Overlook a space of flowers,
And the silent isle imbowers
The Lady of Shalott.

By the margin, willow veil'd,
Slide the heavy barges trail'd
By slow horses; and unhail'd
The shallop flitteth silken-sail'd
Skimming down to Camelot:
But who hath seen her wave her hand?
Or at the casement seen her stand?
Or is she known in all the land,
The Lady of Shalott?

Only reapers, reaping early
In among the bearded barley,
Hear a song that echoes cheerly
From the river winding clearly,
Down to tower'd Camelot:
And by the moon the reaper weary,
Piling sheaves in uplands airy,
Listening, whispers "'Tis the fairy
Lady of Shalott."

Part II

There she weaves by night and day
A magic web with colours gay.
She has heard a whisper say,
A curse is on her if she stay
To look down to Camelot.
She knows not what the curse may be,
And so she weaveth steadily,
And little other care hath she,
The Lady of Shalott.

And moving thro' a mirror clear
That hangs before her all the year,
Shadows of the world appear.
There she sees the highway near
Winding down to Camelot:
There the river eddy whirls,
And there the surly village-churls,
And the red cloaks of market girls,
Pass onward from Shalott.

Sometimes a troop of damsels glad,
An abbot on an ambling pad,
Sometimes a curly shepherd-lad,
Or long-hair'd page in crimson clad,
Goes by to tower'd Camelot;
And sometimes thro' the mirror blue
The knights come riding two and two:
She hath no loyal knight and true,
The Lady of Shalott.

But in her web she still delights
To weave the mirror's magic sights,
For often thro' the silent nights
A funeral, with plumes and lights
And music, went to Camelot;
Or when the moon was overhead,
Came two young lovers lately wed:
"I am half sick of shadows," said
The Lady of Shalott.

Sir Lancelot

Introduction

In continuation from lesson 5:9, students focus on part three of 'The Lady of Shalott' and examine how Lord Tennyson describes the character of Sir Lancelot. After analysing the linguistics and semantics used, they scrutinise the final stanza of part three and consider how structure and pace have been used for effect.

Aims and objectives

- Explain how specific choices and combinations of form, layout and presentation create particular effects.
- Select techniques and devices used by writers, and draw on a range of evidence, opinions, information and the purpose of the task, in order to develop a consistent viewpoint in their own non-fiction writing.

Starter (5 minutes)

Share any prior knowledge of the figure of Sir Lancelot (www.sir-lancelot.co.uk) and recap events and characters from 'The Lady of Shalott' (from lesson 5:9).

Main phase (40 minutes)

- Introduce the learning objectives and lesson outcomes: to analyse Lord Tennyson's use of linguistic and structural devices for effect.
- Read the first section of part three of the poem in which Sir Lancelot is introduced. Ask students to highlight positive vocabulary used to describe this figure, for example 'glittered', 'dazzled' and 'sparkled', and discuss how these words are connected.
- Students write a paragraph analysing Tennyson's use of language for effect, commenting on the patterns of description that they have noticed across the stanzas.

Plenary (15 minutes)

Read the final stanza of part three together and discuss the questions on the task sheet relating to the Lady's motives and the poet's use of structure and pace for effect.

Homework ideas

Ask students to create a DVD cover for a new film based on the Lady of Shalott and Sir Lancelot. Remind them to include a blurb and pictures of the actor and actress they have chosen to play the leading roles.

Make it easier!

Model the annotation and analysis task.

Make it harder!

Introduce the term 'semantic field' (www.urbandictionary.com/define.php?term=Semantic %20field) to students to stretch their understanding of linguistic patterns with the multiple references to the solar system in part three, e.g. 'meteor', 'galaxy', 'starry clusters', and explore the effects of this group of vocabulary.

5:10 Sir Lancelot

1. Sir Lancelot, one of the most famous knights in Arthurian legend, features in the second half of 'The Lady of Shalott'. Read the description of him in part three of the poem and highlight positive words that are used to describe him.

   Part III

   A bow-shot from her bower-eaves,
   He rode between the barley-sheaves,
   The sun came dazzling thro' the leaves,
   And flamed upon the brazen greaves
   Of bold Sir Lancelot.
   A red-cross knight for ever kneel'd
   To a lady in his shield,
   That sparkled on the yellow field,
   Beside remote Shalott.

   The gemmy bridle glitter'd free,
   Like to some branch of stars we see
   Hung in the golden Galaxy.
   The bridle bells rang merrily
   As he rode down to Camelot:
   And from his blazon'd baldric slung
   A mighty silver bugle hung,
   And as he rode his armour rung,
   Beside remote Shalott.

   All in the blue unclouded weather
   Thick-jewell'd shone the saddle-leather,
   The helmet and the helmet-feather
   Burn'd like one burning flame together,
   As he rode down to Camelot.
   As often thro' the purple night,
   Below the starry clusters bright,
   Some bearded meteor, trailing light,
   Moves over still Shalott.

   His broad clear brow in sunlight glow'd;
   On burnish'd hooves his war-horse trode;
   From underneath his helmet flow'd
   His coal-black curls as on he rode,
   As he rode down to Camelot.
   From the bank and from the river
   He flash'd into the crystal mirror,
   "Tirra lirra," by the river
   Sang Sir Lancelot.

2. Consider how the words that you have highlighted make Sir Lancelot sound rich, powerful and bedazzling. What language patterns do you notice? Write a paragraph explaining how Lord Tennyson has used language for effect in this passage of the poem, analysing your selected quotes in detail.

3. Now read the final stanza of part three which focuses on the Lady of Shalott's reaction to seeing Sir Lancelot, and then answer the questions below.

   She left the web, she left the loom,
   She made three paces thro' the room,
   She saw the water-lily bloom,
   She saw the helmet and the plume,
   She look'd down to Camelot.
   Out flew the web and floated wide;
   The mirror crack'd from side to side;
   "The curse is come upon me," cried
   The Lady of Shalott.

   What do you think causes her to leave the room?

   How is this stanza different from all of the others in the poem so far?

   What do you notice about the pace of this stanza? What is the poet trying to show?

Camelot News

Introduction

In continuation from lessons 5:9 and 5:10, students read the last part of 'The Lady of Shalott' and consolidate their understanding of the poem by creating a news bulletin reporting the key events. Students work in groups to devise and perform the *Camelot News*, focusing on their need to use authentic Standard English in role.

Aims and objectives

- Make some appropriate selections from a range of conventions and forms in speech.
- Use standard English, adapting the level of formality to different situations.

Starter (10 minutes)

Ask students to identify four key events or pieces of information from 'The Lady of Shalott' so far and add a sketch and sentence to explain these scenes in the storyboard on their task sheets. Share and compare.

Main phase (35 minutes)

- Introduce the learning objectives and lesson outcomes: to read the final part of the poem and perform a news bulletin, in groups, reporting the events that occur in the poem.
- Read part four of 'The Lady of Shalott', pausing to check understanding and meaning. Students select two more scenes to add to their storyboard from the end of the poem.
- Organise students into groups and ask them to designate roles for themselves, including news anchor, on-the-scene reporter and eye witnesses. Students then discuss and plan the contents of their news reports, being careful to get a good balance of scripted and improvised dialogue to make the performance authentic.

Plenary (15 minutes)

Students perform their news bulletins to the rest of the class, focusing on the quality and appropriateness of the English and the body language they use in role. Evaluate performances.

Homework ideas

Ask students to create the front page for *The Camelot Times*, reporting the mysterious death of the Lady of Shalott.

Make it easier!

Watch a clip of local or national news on the internet to familiarise students with the format of these kinds of reports. Identify key features that students should aim to include in their own bulletins.

Make it harder!

Ask students to write a critical review of their own performances.

5:11 Camelot news

1. Reflect on the events of the first three parts of 'The Lady of Shalott' and choose six important scenes from the poem. Sketch them in the first four boxes of the storyboard below and accompany with a caption.

2. Read part four of the poem and then add the final two scenes to your storyboard.

Part IV

In the stormy east-wind straining,
The pale yellow woods were waning,
The broad stream in his banks complaining,
Heavily the low sky raining
Over tower'd Camelot;
Down she came and found a boat
Beneath a willow left afloat,
And round about the prow she wrote
The Lady of Shalott.

And down the river's dim expanse
Like some bold seer in a trance,
Seeing all his own mischance
With a glassy countenance
Did she look to Camelot.
And at the closing of the day
She loosed the chain, and down she lay;
The broad stream bore her far away,
The Lady of Shalott.

Lying, robed in snowy white
That loosely flew to left and right
The leaves upon her falling light
Thro' the noises of the night
She floated down to Camelot:
And as the boat-head wound along
The willowy hills and fields among,
They heard her singing her last song,
The Lady of Shalott.

Heard a carol, mournful, holy,
Chanted loudly, chanted lowly,
Till her blood was frozen slowly,
And her eyes were darken'd wholly,
Turn'd to tower'd Camelot.
For ere she reach'd upon the tide
The first house by the water-side,
Singing in her song she died,
The Lady of Shalott.

Under tower and balcony,
By garden-wall and gallery,
A gleaming shape she floated by,
Dead-pale between the houses high,
Silent into Camelot.
Out upon the wharfs they came,
Knight and burgher, lord and dame,
And round the prow they read her name,
The Lady of Shalott.

Who is this? And what is here?
And in the lighted palace near
Died the sound of royal cheer;
And they cross'd themselves for fear,
All the knights at Camelot:
But Lancelot mused a little space;
He said, "She has a lovely face;
God in his mercy lend her grace,
The Lady of Shalott."

3. In groups you are now going to prepare and perform an episode of the *Camelot News*, reporting the death of this mysterious lady. In your groups you need to have the following roles covered:

- news anchor

- on-the-scene reporter

- eye witnesses

Goblin Market

Introduction

In this lesson, students are introduced to the poem 'Goblin Market' by Christina Rossetti. After speculating over the title and guessing the content of the poem, students read the opening of the text, focusing on the lush description. Students then write the next stage of the poem, using their own imaginative ideas.

Aims and objectives

- Explore, problem-solve, connect and shape ideas, and identify the most appropriate approach to planning their writing.
- Explore how different audiences choose and respond to texts.

Starter (10 minutes)

Introduce the title of the poem 'Goblin Market'. Students predict and discuss what this title might be referring to. They create their own ideas and note these down on the task sheet.

Main phase (40 minutes)

- Introduce the learning objectives and lesson outcomes: to engage with the description in the opening of Christina Rossetti's poem and then develop their own alternative ending for the text.
- Read the opening of 'Goblin Market' and ask students to highlight all of the fruits that are listed. Discuss the vocabulary used to describe the fruits and ask students to comment on Rossetti's use of language and form on their task sheets.
- Students then read the next section of the poem and speculate on what might happen next, knowing that speaking to the goblins is prohibited and Lizzie seems curious. Students plan their own ideas for the ending of the poem and start to draft them.

Plenary (10 minutes)

Ask students to share their poem ending ideas in pairs and reveal the best ones to the rest of the class.

Homework ideas

Ask students to design their own goblin for sale and create an eBay advert, including a product description.

Make it easier!

Review images inspired by the poem, which can be found on the internet.

Make it harder!

Stretch students by getting them to consider parallels with the ideas of forbidden fruit found in the Bible.

5:12 Goblin Market

1. Consider the title 'Goblin Market' and guess what you think it refers to. What sort of place is this? What happens there? Describe your ideas in the box below.

> Goblin Market

2. Now read the opening of this poem, written by Christina Rossetti. Identify all of the fruits listed in the text and circle/highlight them. What kind of description is provided? What impression does the reader get of the goblins' goods? Write your ideas in the box below.

Goblin Market

Morning and evening
Maids heard the goblins cry:
"Come buy our orchard fruits,
Come buy, come buy:
Apples and quinces,
Lemons and oranges,
Plump unpeck'd cherries,
Melons and raspberries,
Bloom-down-cheek'd peaches,
Swart-headed mulberries,
Wild free-born cranberries,
Crab-apples, dewberries,
Pine-apples, blackberries,
Apricots, strawberries; –
All ripe together
In summer weather, –

Morns that pass by,
Fair eves that fly;
Come buy, come buy:
Our grapes fresh from the vine,
Pomegranates full and fine,
Dates and sharp bullaces,
Rare pears and greengages,
Damsons and bilberries,
Taste them and try:
Currants and gooseberries,
Bright-fire-like barberries,
Figs to fill your mouth,
Citrons from the South,
Sweet to tongue and sound to eye;
Come buy, come buy."

3. Read the next part of the poem below and then complete the poem with your own imaginative ideas about what will happen.

Evening by evening
Among the brookside rushes,
Laura bow'd her head to hear,
Lizzie veil'd her blushes:
Crouching close together
In the cooling weather,
With clasping arms and cautioning lips,
With tingling cheeks and finger tips.

"Lie close," Laura said,
Pricking up her golden head:
"We must not look at goblin men,
We must not buy their fruits:
Who knows upon what soil they fed
Their hungry thirsty roots?"
"Come buy," call the goblins
Hobbling down the glen.

The Globe

Introduction
In this lesson, students will develop their understanding of Shakespeare's theatre by sharing prior knowledge and researching The Globe. They will use the internet to source information about the theatre and present this in the form of an educational poster for display.

Aims and objectives
- Make relevant notes in a range of formats and approaches when researching a variety of sources.
- Select the most appropriate text format, layout and presentation to create impact and engage the reader.

Starter (10 minutes)
Introduce the word 'globe' and ask students to generate a list of things that they associate with the term. Focus on the theatre on the river bank in London and ask students to share any information that they know about it. Why was it called The Globe? When was it built? Which famous playwright is associated with it? Students create notes on their task sheets.

For more information visit:

www.shakespeares-globe.org/abouttheglobe/background/thefirstglobe/

Main phase (45 minutes)
- Introduce the learning objectives and lesson task: to research Shakespeare's theatre and produce an educational poster filled with facts about The Globe and pictures of it to be displayed.
- Students use internet search engines to source appropriate information to include on their posters; prompts are available on the task sheet. They plan the poster layout on the task sheet and make notes from their findings.
- Once students have gathered enough material (facts as well as images), they start to create their poster on paper or using the computer.

Reflection (5 minutes)
Peer-evaluate posters; students judge according to the quality of information and presentation.

Homework ideas
Ask students to complete their Globe posters for display.

Make it easier!
Show students pictures of The Globe theatre in the starter (available on Google images).

Make it harder!
Ask students to include information about Elizabethan theatres such as The Rose and The Swan.

6:1 The Globe

1. Use the circle below to make notes about Shakespeare's theatre, The Globe. Write down facts that you learn from other members of your class and through your research.

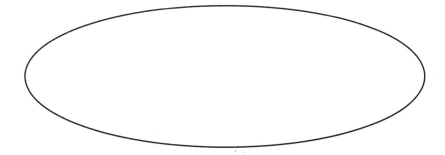

2. You are going to be making an educational poster about The Globe theatre. While researching the web, try to find out the answers to the following questions. These could be included in your poster.

   • When was it built?

   • Why was it named The Globe?

   • What shape is the stage and the auditorium?

   • Why did performances depend on daylight and good weather?

   • What types of plays were performed there?

   • When was it closed, and why?

   • When was it rebuilt, and why?

3. Now design the layout and content of your poster in the space opposite.

4. Review at least two other posters and make notes about the quality of their information, content and presentation in the spaces below.

   . . . .
   . . . .
   . . . .
   . . . .
   . . . .
   . . . .
   . . . .

A Midsummer Night's Dream

Introduction

This lesson involves pre-reading activities that introduce students to Shakespeare's *A Midsummer Night's Dream*. Students focus on the connotations of the words in the play's title and then create their own play synopsis using a list of ingredients from the original text.

Aims and objectives

- Use a repertoire of reading strategies to analyse and explore different layers of meaning within texts.
- Establish and sustain distinctive character, point of view and voice in their fiction writing by drawing on a wide range of techniques and devices used by writers.

Starter (10 minutes)

Students use their inference skills to discuss and make notes about each of the words in the play's title and predict its themes and events. Share and compare ideas.

Main phase (40 minutes)

- Introduce the learning objectives and lesson outcomes: to create a synopsis for a play of the same title using common ingredients.
- Students look at the list of ingredients and, using their imaginations, discuss how they might feature in a play entitled *A Midsummer Night's Dream*.
- Once students have generated their ideas and devised a plot line utilizing all of the ingredients, they start to write either a detailed synopsis or a script for their play.

Plenary (10 minutes)

Students turn their ideas into a film trailer voice-over and perform these to the rest of the class. Discuss and evaluate ideas.

Homework ideas

Ask students to create a poster advertising their play, including plot details.

Make it easier!

Discuss and share possible storylines, creating the ingredients with reference to fairy tales and fantasy films such as *Shrek* to help students to generate their ideas.

Make it harder!

Ask students to work in groups to create a performance of one of their plays to show to the rest of the class in the plenary.

6:2 A Midsummer Night's Dream

1. Focus on each word in the title below and write down associations and ideas of meanings around each one.

Midsummer   Night   Dream

2. From your connotations, predict the themes and events that take place in this Shakespeare play and write your suggestions in the box below.

3. Using the following ingredients, create your own synopsis for a play entitled *A Midsummer Night's Dream*. Use your imagination and try to make the plot entertaining. Plan your ideas in the box below.

lovers

potion

donkey

forest

King and Queen

fairies

wedding

actors

© Helena Ceranic, 2011. *Resources for Teaching English: 11–14.*

Parental problems

Introduction

In this lesson, students focus on an extract from the opening of *A Midsummer Night's Dream* in which Hermia argues against her father's plans for an arranged marriage with Demetrius. Students write agony aunt letters in role as one of the characters and respond to each other with advice.

Aims and objectives

- Develop an understanding of how ideas, experiences and values are portrayed in texts from different cultures and traditions.
- Write fluently and sustain standard English in wide and varied texts and contexts, and for a range of purposes and audiences.

Starter (10 minutes)

Introduce the concept of arranged marriages and ask students to share their views on this tradition. Students note down reasons for and against on their task sheets. Discuss how attitudes towards love and marriage differ according to historical period or religious faith.

Main phase (35 minutes)

- Introduce the learning objectives and outcomes: to consider Hermia's dilemma in *A Midsummer Night's Dream* and write agony aunt letters and responses in role.
- Read the extract from the play and clarify the characters' circumstances (Egeus, Hermia's father has chosen Demetrius as her love match. Hermia is in love with Lysander and has refused to follow her father's orders. Egeus has taken them to see the Duke of Athens to enforce his decision; if Hermia refuses to follow her father's will, she could lose her life).
- After discussing how Hermia, Egeus, Lysander and Demetrius would feel in this scene, students pick one of the characters and write a letter to an agony aunt in role. They should explain their feelings and sense of injustice.

Plenary (15 minutes)

Students swap letters and draft responses in role as the agony aunt or uncle. Ask them what advice they would give to the character in question.

Homework ideas

Ask students to research women's rights and marriage in Elizabethan England and write a paragraph explaining how society has changed its views since the sixteenth/seventeenth century.

Make it easier!

Provide students with a writing frame to help them to structure their agony aunt letters, e.g.

Paragraph 1: State the problems you are experiencing.

Paragraph 2: Explain how it is making you feel and what you have considered doing.

Paragraph 3: Ask for help and advice.

Make it harder!

Challenge students to use old-fashioned language in their letters to make them sound authentic.

6:3 Parental problems

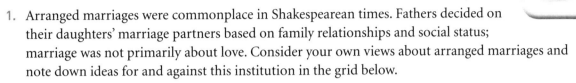

1. Arranged marriages were commonplace in Shakespearean times. Fathers decided on their daughters' marriage partners based on family relationships and social status; marriage was not primarily about love. Consider your own views about arranged marriages and note down ideas for and against this institution in the grid below.

Arguments for arranged marriages	Arguments against arranged marriages

2. Now read the abridged extract from the opening of *A Midummer Night's Dream* in which Egeus (Hermia's father) takes his daughter to see Theseus (the Duke of Athens). Egeus complains that Hermia refuses to marry the husband that he has chosen for her (Demetrius) and is outraged by her wish to marry another Athenian, Lysander.

> **EGEUS:** Happy be Theseus!
>
> Full of vexation come I, with complaint against my daughter Hermia. Stand forth, Demetrius!
>
> *(Demetrius steps forward.)*
>
> My noble lord, this man hath my consent to marry her.
>
> Stand forth, Lysander!
>
> *(Lysander steps forward.)*
>
> And this man hath bewitched my child.
>
> If she will not marry Demetrius as I wish, I will use the ancient law of Athens, which says: as she is my daughter I may dispose of her, either to this gentleman or to her death.
>
> **THESEUS:** Be advised, fair maid. Demetrius is a worthy gentleman.
>
> **HERMIA:** So is Lysander! I beg your grace to tell me the worst that may befall me in this case if I refuse to wed Demetrius.
>
> **THESEUS:** Either to die the death, or never see another man again. Take time to think.
>
> **LYSANDER:** I am my lord as well derived as Demetrius, and, which is more, I am beloved of beauteous Hermia. Demetrius loves Helena!
>
> **THESEUS:** Enough! Demetrius and Egeus come with me. For you, fair Hermia, look you fit your fancies to your father's will.
>
> *Theseus and Hippolyta depart followed by Egeus and Demetrius.*

> **LYSANDER:** The course of true love never did run smooth.
>
> If thou lovest me,
>
> Then steal from thy father's house tomorrow night,
>
> And in the wood, a league out of the town, there will I stay for thee.
>
> There, gentle Hermia, may I marry thee;
>
> And to that place the sharp Athenian law
>
> Cannot pursue us.
>
> **HERMIA:** I swear to thee by Cupid's strongest bow,
>
> Tomorrow truly will I meet with thee!
>
> **LYSANDER:** Keep promise, love. Look here comes Helena!

3. Choose one of the characters from this scene who is angry and needs advice about what to do. Write a letter in role to an agony aunt explaining your problems and asking for their support.

4. Now swap letters and write a response, giving advice in role as the agony aunt or uncle.

Shakespearean comedy

Introduction

In this lesson, students explore the features of Shakespearean comedy. After sharing their own understanding of this genre, they research synopses from a range of different Shakespearean comedies to identify the central facets of comedy in Shakespeare's time period. They then produce the wedding announcement pages for *The Shakespeare Times*, reporting the marriages that occur at the end of the plays.

Aims and objectives

- Select from a range of strategies and use the most appropriate ways to locate, retrieve and compare information and ideas from a variety of texts.
- Make relevant notes in a range of formats and approaches when researching a variety of sources.

Starter (10 minutes)

Introduce the term 'comedy' and ask students to share what they understand about this genre. What sorts of things happen in comedy films? What kind of characters do comedy films contain? Then explain that the notion of comedy has changed over the centuries and that Shakespearean comedies are more akin to modern romantic comedies. Students make notes on the task sheet about what they understand by the rom-com genre.

Main phase (35 minutes)

- Introduce the learning objectives and lesson outcomes: to identify the features of Shakespearean comedies and write a newspaper announcement reporting the events that occur at the end of *A Midsummer Night's Dream*.
- Students use the internet to research the synopses of some of Shakespeare's most famous comedies: *A Midsummer Night's Dream*, *Twelfth Night* and *Much Ado About Nothing*. They make notes about the plays' plot lines on the task sheet, using websites. Useful websites include:

    www.nosweatshakespeare.com/play-summary.htm
    www.bardweb.net/plays/index.html

- Students review their notes and identify common plot lines that occur in all three plays. They use this information to write their own definition of Shakespearean comedy.

Plenary (15 minutes)

Students then draft the wedding announcement page of *The Shakespeare Times*, reporting the marriages that take place at the end of one of the comedy plays.

Homework ideas

Ask students to create newspaper announcements of the weddings, including images and appropriate presentation.

Make it easier!

Show students wedding announcement pages in a local newspaper to familiarise them with the content and style of this kind of text.

Make it harder!

Ask students to design their wedding article in the style of a *Hello* magazine exclusive spread.

6:4 Shakespearean comedy

1. Write down what you expect to happen in a comedy in the space below. What kinds of things happen in comedy films? What kinds of characters appear in them? Then write down the features of a romantic comedy.

   Comedy:

   Romantic comedy:

2. You are now going to research three of Shakespeare's comedies to identify the features of this genre. Use the internet to find out what happens in the plays below and make notes in the space provided.

Shakespeare comedy	Storyline
A Midsummer Night's Dream	
Twelfth Night	
Much Ado About Nothing	

3. Having found out about the events that occur in these three plays, write down what you understand to be common features of a Shakespearean comedy in the box below.

4. Now you are going to produce the marriage announcement page of *The Shakespeare Times*, using the information you have found about the three plays above. Remember to include the names of all of the characters involved.

Desert island companions

Introduction

This lesson contains pre-reading activities for *The Tempest*. Students complete a desert island discs style starter in which they choose and justify the items that they would select in this scenario. They then discuss pen portraits of the characters from the play and consider the positive and negative attributes these characters would have to offer as island companions.

Aims and objectives

- Move a discussion forward by developing and drawing together ideas arising from discussion.
- Develop interpretations of texts, supporting points with detailed textual evidence.

Starter (10 minutes)

Ask students to imagine that they are marooned on a desert island and consider what objects they would choose to have with them. Students list three items on their task sheet and add explanations. Discuss choices.

Main phase (40 minutes)

- Introduce the learning objectives and lesson outcomes: to find out about the main characters in *The Tempest* and consider what kinds of companions they would make on a desert island.
- Introduce the brief synopsis of *The Tempest* and the four pen portraits on the task sheet. Students read the descriptions and identify the positive and negative traits of each character.
- In groups, students identify which of the four characters would make the best companion on the island and which one they would be least keen to share the island with. They write a persuasive speech arguing for one of the characters to be voted off the island.

Plenary (10 minutes)

Students share their persuasive speeches and take a vote on which character should be thrown out to sea.

Homework ideas

Ask students to watch Shakespeare's *Animated Tales: The Tempest* on YouTube and write a summary of the play.

Make it easier!

Show the class different pictures of the four characters from various productions of the play to extend their appreciation of them (available through Google images).

Make it harder!

Read extracts from Act 1 of *The Tempest* to extend students' understanding of the four characters:

www.shakespeare-online.com/plays/temp_1_2.html

6:5 Desert island companions

1. Imagine that you are stranded on a desert island. What three items would you
   choose to have with you on the island and why? Explain your decisions below.

   1. . . . .

                                                          . . . .

   2. . . . .

                                                          . . . .

   3. . . . .

                                                          . . . .

2. Shakespeare's *The Tempest* is set on a remote island. The following characters are living on the island
   and they are joined by a number of other characters who are shipwrecked there at the start of the
   play.

   Read through the character cards and identify the positive and negative attributes of the characters.
   In your group, decide which character would be most useful as a companion and which character you
   would least like to live alongside.

Prospero

Father of Miranda, Prospero has lived on the island for many years. He used to be Duke
of Milan before he was usurped and abandoned at sea with his daughter, which has
caused him to be bitter and seek revenge. He has magical powers and is able to control
the elements. He is master to Ariel, whom he treats as a servant, and Caliban, whom he
treats like a slave.

Caliban

Caliban is native to the island. His mother Sycorax, a witch, used to control the island.
Caliban is familiar with the island and knows where to get fresh food and water. When
Prospero first arrived on the island he treated Caliban kindly, but since Caliban tried to
rape his daughter, Prospero has tortured Caliban and made him his slave. Caliban is
described as monstrous; half-man, half-fish.

Miranda

Miranda is Prospero's daughter. She came to the island with her father when she was
very young and remembers very little of her life back in Milan. She is naive and has only
ever known her father and Caliban. She is dutiful and compassionate and becomes upset
and emotional when hearing about human suffering.

Ariel

Ariel is an ethereal spirit which does not have a gender. It carries out Prospero's orders since Prospero freed it from a cage when he arrived. Ariel is able to transform itself into any shape or form to trick and confuse others. It seems to take pleasure and pride in the jobs it performs for Prospero. It is an obedient slave but looks forward to its freedom.

3. Once you have made your decision you will argue for your preferred and your least favourite island companion against other members of the class.

Cooking up a storm

> **Resources**
> Large space for drama performance

Introduction

In this lesson, students focus on the storm that takes place in the opening scene of *The Tempest*. Students create a spell for conjuring up a storm and consider how it would have been difficult to achieve this on a Shakespearean stage with no modern special effects. Students then perform the scene from the play, using dramatic techniques to bring the storm to life.

Aims and objectives

- Use a wide variety of dramatic approaches and conventions to analyse complex and challenging ideas, issues, themes and texts.
- Develop and sustain a variety of processes, narratives, performances and roles through the selection and adaptation of appropriate dramatic conventions, techniques and styles.

Starter (15 minutes)

Students discuss the elements and feelings associated with a storm and fill in the spider diagram on their task sheets. They then create Prospero's spell for the storm, using ideas from their spider diagram.

Main phase (30 minutes)

- Introduce the learning objective and lesson outcomes: to study and perform the opening scene of *The Tempest*.
- Read the opening of Act 1, Scene 1 of *The Tempest* and discuss how the fraught exclamations and commands show the stress and anxiety of the situation. Explain that Shakespeare did not have special effects at his disposal and that staging effects were limited.
- Group students and ask them to discuss the storm scene and ways to perform it. Students allocate roles and actions and practise their performances.

Plenary (15 minutes)

Watch storm performances and peer-evaluate, focusing on how successful and inventive groups have been in recreating a storm.

Homework ideas

Ask students to research the plot line of *The Tempest* and write a summary.

Make it easier!

Watch the opening of a film version of the play to consider how the storm in Act 1 has been presented.

Make it harder!

Discuss the status of the different characters in the opening scene and how positions of power have been subverted in this emergency situation.

6:6 Cooking up a storm

1. The opening of Shakespeare's *The Tempest* starts with a strong storm that is the cause of the shipwreck. Complete the spider diagram below with things and feelings that you associate with storms.

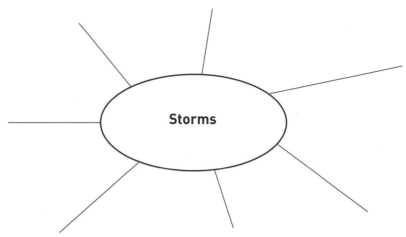

2. Soon into Act 1 we learn that the storm is not a natural occurance but was created by Prospero using his magic powers. Using ideas from your spider diagram above, create Prospero's spell for making the storm.

   Now read the opening of Act 1, Scene 1 in which the storm takes place. You are then going to perform this scene, bringing the storm to life by using a range of imaginative dramatic techniques.

ACT I SCENE I

On a ship at sea: a tempestuous noise of thunder and lightning heard. Enter a Master and a Boatswain

Master: Boatswain!

Boatswain: Here, master: what cheer?

Master: Good, speak to the mariners: fall to't, yarely, or we run ourselves aground: bestir, bestir.

Exit

Enter Mariners

Boatswain: Heigh, my hearts! cheerly, cheerly, my hearts! yare, yare! Take in the topsail. Tend to the master's whistle. Blow, till thou burst thy wind, if room enough!

Enter ALONSO, SEBASTIAN, ANTONIO, FERDINAND, GONZALO, and others.

ALONSO: Good boatswain, have care. Where's the master? Play the men.

Boatswain: I pray now, keep below.

ANTONIO: Where is the master, boatswain?

Boatswain: Do you not hear him? You mar our labour: keep your cabins: you do assist the storm.

What makes a monster?

Introduction

In this lesson, students explore the definition of monstrosity with a focus on the character of Caliban from *The Tempest*. They examine quotations from the text in which Caliban is described or treated like a monster and discuss the implications of these judgements. They then create a monologue in the voice of Caliban.

Aims and objectives

- Analyse and respond to the range of ideas and differing viewpoints, purposes and themes in a variety of related texts.
- Establish and sustain distinctive character, point of view and voice in their fiction writing by drawing on a wide range of techniques and devices used by writers.

Starter (10 minutes)

Introduce the term 'monster' and ask students to share their interpretations of this word. Students look up the word in a dictionary and write down different meanings and associations of monstrosity on the task sheet.

Main phase (40 minutes)

- Introduce the learning objectives and lesson outcomes: to explore the notion of monstrosity in relation to the character of Caliban and write a monologue communicating the creature's feelings about his treatment.
- Look at the various quotes taken from the text that describe the character of Caliban. Students make notes around each, considering the evidence of his monstrosity.
- Students then reflect on how Caliban would feel being treated like a monster. They write a monologue for his character, exploring his thoughts and frustrations.

Plenary (10 minutes)

Individual students share lines from their monologues with the rest of the class. Discuss how society has a part to play in how monstrosity is defined.

Homework ideas

Ask students to create a monster collage with pictures and words that they associate with monstrosity.

Make it easier!

Provide students with a writing frame or prompts to support their monologue writing, e.g.: What do you think of Prospero? What would you like to change about your life on the island? What upsets you?

Make it harder!

Ask students to consider the implications of the name 'Caliban' being an anagram of 'canibal'. Discuss the meaning of this word and introduce Michael de Montaigne's theory:

> Michel de Montaigne's essay 'Of cannibals' introduced a new multicultural note in European civilization. Montaigne wrote that 'one calls "barbarism" whatever he is not accustomed to'.

6:7 What makes a monster?

1. Discuss the term 'monster'. What does this word make you think of? Using a dictionary, write down a definition of monstrosity in the box below.

> **Monstrosity**

2. In *The Tempest* Caliban is considered to be a monster by all the characters that he comes into contact with. Read the quotations taken from the text below and, reflecting on your definitions of monstrosity, make notes about the kind of language used by Caliban or to describe him. Consider how he is treated and how he behaves.

> **Prospero:** Thou poisonous slave, got by the devil himself

> **Caliban:** You taught me language; and my profit on't is, I know how to curse.

> **Trinculo:** What have we here, a man or a fish? Dead or alive?

> **Stephano:** This is some monster of the isle with four legs

> **Caliban:** Do not torment me, prithee; I'll bring my wood home faster.

> **Caliban:** I'll show thee every fertile inch o' th' island
> And I will kiss thy foot: I prithee, be my god.

> **Caliban:** Having first seized his books, or with a log,
> Batter his skull, or paunch him with a stake

3. In role as Caliban, write a monologue explaining the way you feel about being treated like a monster. Refer to the above quotes in your writing.

All hail Macbeth!

Introduction

In this lesson, students reflect on how witches are perceived in society and focus on Macbeth and Banquo's encounter with the three hags in the play. After examining the extract in which the witches predict the men's futures, students write a diary entry as one of the characters, reflecting on the event that has just occurred.

Aims and objectives

- Develop an understanding of how ideas, experiences and values are portrayed in texts from different cultures and traditions.
- Establish and sustain a clear and logical personal viewpoint through the analysis and selection of convincing evidence, opinions and appropriate information, and other techniques used by writers to meet the purpose of the task.

Starter (10 minutes)

Ask students to consider a stereotypical image of a witch and draw and label their ideas on the task sheet. Share students' understanding of witchcraft and discuss how perceptions and treatment of witches have changed over time.

Main phase (35 minutes)

- Introduce the learning objectives and lesson outcomes: to analyse a scene from *Macbeth* in which Macbeth and Banquo encounter three witches, and write in role, explaining how the character feels after this event.
- Read the extract from Macbeth together. Discuss and identify the predictions that the witches make about the two characters' futures and highlight how Macbeth and Banquo respond to the witches.
- Students consider how Banquo and Macbeth would feel after being told by the witches that the future has great things in store for them. Would they believe them? Would they be suspicious? How would this knowledge affect their behaviour?

Plenary (15 minutes)

Students write a diary entry in role as Banquo or Macbeth that evening, including their feelings and reactions to their encounter with the witches.

Homework ideas

Ask students to find out why it is unlucky to say the name 'Macbeth' inside the theatre and write a paragraph about the superstitious 'curse of Macbeth'.

Make it easier!

Ask students to complete the plenary activity in groups to enable them to share ideas.

Make it harder!

Give students the opportunity to research witchcraft throughout the centuries.

6:8 All hail Macbeth!

1. Shakespeare's *Macbeth* opens with a famous scene in which three witches make plans to meet again. Draw a stereotypical image of a witch below and label it with the traditional physical and behavioural features you expect witches to have.

2. In Shakespeare's time witches were believed to be spawned from the devil and were deeply mistrusted and feared. In Act 1, Scene 3 Macbeth and his fellow soldier Banquo bump into three witches when returning from battle. The witches make predictions about both men's futures that unsettle them. Read the extract below and highlight the phrases that show the witches' predictions and how the men react to them.

> **MACBETH:** Speak, if you can: what are you?
>
> **First Witch:** All hail, Macbeth! hail to thee, thane of Glamis!
>
> **Second Witch:** All hail, Macbeth, hail to thee, thane of Cawdor!
>
> **Third Witch:** All hail, Macbeth, thou shalt be king hereafter!
>
> **BANQUO:** Good sir, why do you start; and seem to fear
>
> Things that do sound so fair? I' the name of truth,
>
> Are ye fantastical, or that indeed
>
> Which outwardly ye show? My noble partner
>
> You greet with present grace and great prediction
>
> Of noble having and of royal hope,
>
> That he seems rapt withal: to me you speak not.
>
> If you can look into the seeds of time,
>
> And say which grain will grow and which will not,
>
> Speak then to me, who neither beg nor fear
>
> Your favours nor your hate.

First Witch: Hail!

Second Witch: Hail!

Third Witch: Hail!

First Witch: Lesser than Macbeth, and greater.

Second Witch: Not so happy, yet much happier.

Third Witch: Thou shalt get kings, though thou be none:

So all hail, Macbeth and Banquo!

First Witch: Banquo and Macbeth, all hail!

MACBETH: Stay, you imperfect speakers, tell me more:

By Sinel's death I know I am thane of Glamis;

But how of Cawdor? the thane of Cawdor lives,

A prosperous gentleman; and to be king

Stands not within the prospect of belief,

No more than to be Cawdor. Say from whence

You owe this strange intelligence? or why

Upon this blasted heath you stop our way

With such prophetic greeting? Speak, I charge you.

Witches vanish

3. Now write a diary entry as Macbeth or Banquo reflecting on their meeting with the witches.

Lady Macbeth

Introduction

In this lesson, students analyse Lady Macbeth's powers of persuasion. They read a passage from the play in which she attempts to convince her husband to kill the king. Students then create an improvised dialogue, modernising the conversation that occurs between the couple to consolidate their understanding of this scene.

Aims and objectives

- Develop and choose effectively from a repertoire of verbal and non-verbal techniques which actively involve listeners.
- Develop and sustain a variety of processes, narratives, performances and roles through the selection and adaptation of appropriate dramatic conventions, techniques and styles.

Starter (10 minutes)

Discuss the range of persuasive techniques listed on the task sheet and consider which ones would have most impact when trying to get your own way. Students rank the techniques in discussion of their own experiences.

Main phase (35 minutes)

- Introduce the learning objectives and lesson outcomes: to understand the persuasive arguments Lady Macbeth uses and how Macbeth reacts to these through re-enacting their argument.
- Contextualise the scene from the play: Lady Macbeth is consumed with ambition to become the Queen of Scotland, as the witches prophesised, and attempts to manipulate Macbeth and convince him to kill King Duncan so that he can step up to the throne.
- Read the passage together and discuss the meaning of any difficult vocabulary and phrasing.
- Through discussion, students identify phrases that exhibit Lady Macbeth's use of persuasive devices. Share findings.

Plenary (15 minutes)

In pairs, without using the play script, students re-enact this scene in role as Macbeth and Lady Macbeth. They need to demonstrate understanding of how Lady Macbeth tries to get her own way and how Macbeth responds to her persuasion.

Homework ideas

Ask students to write a paragraph explaining which actress they would cast as Lady Macbeth, in a new production of the play, and why.

Make it easier!

Watch this scene in Roman Polanski's version of *Macbeth* to consider how the actress playing Lady Macbeth, Francesca Annis, portrays the character's manipulative attitude (available on YouTube).

Make it harder!

Ask students to create soliloquies as Lady Macbeth for the plenary activity.

6:9 Lady Macbeth

1. In *Macbeth*, Lady Macbeth is a very persuasive character. Look at the range of persuasive techniques below and rank them in order of effectiveness. Which devices are most likely to help you to convince someone to do what you want them to?

   - promises
   - the imperative
   - threats/dares
   - emotional blackmail
   - repetition
   - constrasting pairs

2. Read the extract below in which Lady Macbeth is trying to convince her husband to kill King Duncan in the hope that this will free a path for her to become the Queen of Scotland. Identify the various techniques that Lady Macbeth uses to persuade Macbeth to do as she wants.

> **LADY MACBETH:** Was the hope drunk
> Wherein you dress'd yourself? Hath it slept since?
> And wakes it now, to look so green and pale
> At what it did so freely? From this time
> Such I account thy love. Art thou afeard
> To be the same in thine own act and valour
> As thou art in desire? Wouldst thou have that
> Which thou esteem'st the ornament of life,
> And live a coward in thine own esteem,
> Letting 'I dare not' wait upon 'I would,'
> Like the poor cat i' the adage?
> **MACBETH:** Prithee, peace:
> I dare do all that may become a man;
> Who dares do more is none.

LADY MACBETH: What beast was't, then,

That made you break this enterprise to me?

When you durst do it, then you were a man;

And, to be more than what you were, you would

Be so much more the man. Nor time nor place

Did then adhere, and yet you would make both:

They have made themselves, and that their fitness now

Does unmake you. I have given suck, and know

How tender 'tis to love the babe that milks me:

I would, while it was smiling in my face,

Have pluck'd my nipple from his boneless gums,

And dash'd the brains out, had I so sworn as you

Have done to this.

MACBETH: If we should fail?

LADY MACBETH: We fail!

But screw your courage to the sticking-place,

And we'll not fail. When Duncan is asleep –

Whereto the rather shall his day's hard journey

Soundly invite him – his two chamberlains

Will I with wine and wassail so convince

That memory, the warder of the brain,

Shall be a fume, and the receipt of reason

A limbeck only: when in swinish sleep

Their drenched natures lie as in a death,

What cannot you and I perform upon

The unguarded Duncan? What not put upon

His spongy officers, who shall bear the guilt

Of our great quell?

3. Now, in pairs, re-enact this argument between Lady Macbeth and Macbeth, focusing on the techniques that she uses to get her own way and the way in which Macbeth responds to her attempts.

Star-crossed lovers

Introduction

In this lesson, students focus on the prologue from *Romeo and Juliet* and identify the features of this Shakespearean tragedy. After turning the text into Standard English, they create a diagram using the list of characters from the play and consider Shakespeare's motivations for outlining the play's events at the start.

Aims and objectives

- Consider how and why the English language has developed as shown in texts from different historical periods up to the present day.
- Analyse how texts are shaped by audiences' preferences and opinions.

Starter (10 minutes)

Ask students to read the prologue from Shakespeare's *Romeo and Juliet* on the task sheet and identify five facts about the play that are communicated to the audience in this introduction. Share and compare findings.

Main phase (40 minutes)

- Introduce the learning objectives and lesson outcomes: to understand the contents and purpose of the prologue and familiarise themselves with the family networks within the play.
- Students reread the prologue and translate the text into Standard English. An example is:

  http://nfs.sparknotes.com/romeojuliet/page_2.html

- Discuss ways in which language and syntax have changed over time.
- Introduce the list of characters from the play and the main households of Capulet and Montague. Students create a diagram to demonstrate the links between the characters.

Plenary (10 minutes)

Ask students to consider why Shakespeare often used prologues in his plays. Discuss the benefits and drawbacks of a chorus introducing the play's setting and events in this way.

Homework ideas

Ask students to write a prologue for a film of their choice, introducing the setting, characters and events.

Make it easier!

Watch the opening of Baz Luhrmann's *Romeo and Juliet* to evaluate how the director has used the prologue in the style of a news report to bring the audience up to speed with the play's setting.

Make it harder!

Discuss the role of the chorus, how it originated in Greek theatre and how it relates to modern theatre conventions, e.g. the narrator in pantomimes. For information see:

www2.selu.edu/Academics/Faculty/jwiemelt/classes/engl230/chorus.htm/

6:10 Star-crossed lovers

1. One of Shakespeare's most famous plays, *Romeo and Juliet*, begins with a prologue spoken by the chorus which introduces the play's setting and events.

   Read the text below and identify five pieces of information that are communicated to the audience.

   > Two households, both alike in dignity,
   > In fair Verona, where we lay our scene,
   > From ancient grudge break to new mutiny,
   > Where civil blood makes civil hands unclean.
   > From forth the fatal loins of these two foes
   > A pair of star-cross'd lovers take their life;
   > Whole misadventured piteous overthrows
   > Do with their death bury their parents' strife.
   > The fearful passage of their death-mark'd love,
   > And the continuance of their parents' rage,
   > Which, but their children's end, nought could remove,
   > Is now the two hours' traffic of our stage;
   > The which if you with patient ears attend,
   > What here shall miss, our toil shall strive to mend.

2. Now attempt to translate the prologue into modern Standard English. You will need to change phrasing and vocabulary but try to retain the same meaning and information. Draft your version of the prologue in the box below.

3. Now look at the list of characters that feature in the play below. Design a diagram showing the links and relationships between all of the characters.

> **List of characters**
>
> **Romeo:** The son of Lord and Lady Montague.
>
> **Juliet:** The daughter of Lord and Lady Capulet.
>
> **Friar Lawrence:** A friar, friend to both Romeo and Juliet.
>
> **Mercutio:** A kinsman to the Prince and Romeo's close friend.
>
> **Nurse:** A nurse who has cared for Juliet her entire life.
>
> **Tybalt:** A Capulet, Juliet's cousin on her mother's side.
>
> **Capulet:** The patriarch of the Capulet family, father of Juliet, husband of Lady Capulet, and enemy, for unexplained reasons, of Montague.
>
> **Lady Capulet:** Juliet's mother, Capulet's wife.
>
> **Montague:** Romeo's father, the patriarch of the Montague clan and bitter enemy of Capulet.
>
> **Lady Montague:** Romeo's mother, Montague's wife.
>
> **Paris:** A kinsman of the Prince, and Capulet's chosen suitor for Juliet.
>
> **Benvolio:** Montague's nephew, Romeo's cousin and friend.
>
> **Prince Escalus:** The Prince of Verona, a kinsman of Mercutio and Paris.
>
> **Balthasar:** Romeo's dedicated servant.
>
> **Sampson and Gregory:** Two servants of the house of Capulet.
>
> **Abram:** Montague's servant.
>
> **Rosaline:** The woman with whom Romeo is infatuated at the beginning of the play.

Ancient grudges

Introduction

In this lesson, students explore the conflict between the two families in *Romeo and Juliet*. After creating their own Shakespearean insults and examining the kind of abusive language used by various characters in Act 1, they create a dialogue between Lord Montague and Lord Capulet, considering their reactions to the Prince's threats.

Aims and objectives

- Analyse and exemplify the way that forms and varieties of English used by speakers and writers can be influenced by context and purpose.
- Use sustained standard English with the degree of formality suited to listeners and purpose.

Starter (10 minutes)

Students construct their own Shakespearean-style insults using the grid of words on the task sheet. They discuss the source of this abusive language, considering how the vocabulary degrades the victim by referring to base and animalistic features and behaviour.

Main phase (35 minutes)

- Introduce the learning objectives and lesson outcomes: to analyse the verbal abuse used by the opposing families in *Romeo and Juliet* and script a dialogue for the two heads of household.
- Read the extract from Act 1, Scene 1 exemplifying the verbal insults taking place. Students identify the derogatory and antagonistic language and discuss.
- Students then consider how Lord Montague and Lord Capulet would feel after their address from Prince Escalus. They script a dialogue between the two characters in order to explore their reactions to the conflict in Act 1 and to the Prince's threats of death.

Plenary (15 minutes)

Hear a range of the scripted dialogues and discuss students' interpretations of these characters' responses.

Homework ideas

Ask students to write a paragraph with examples of 'ancient grudges' that still exist in society (e.g. North vs. South, English vs. French, Manchester United vs. Manchester City) and the reasons for their existence.

Make it easier!

Start to script the dialogue together as a class.

Make it harder!

Read the whole of Act 1, Scene 1, available online, to broaden students' understanding and knowledge of this scene.

Unit 6: Engaging with Shakespeare   TEACHER SHEET

6:11 Ancient grudges

1. The prologue to *Romeo and Juliet* informs the audience of a long-standing grudge between the Capulet and Montague households. In the first scene of the play we witness servants from the opposing families antagonisinig each other with verbal abuse.

    Create your own Shakespearean insults using the words in the grid blow. What do you notice about the kind of vocabulary that is being using to degrade the opposing party?

Thou art a . . .	crazed dank fiendish harried jittery limp rank	filth-sucking sheep-brained lemon-legged jelly-livered pasty-skinned mould-riddled toad-headed	gibbon nettle grub harlot boar harpy brute codpiece

2. Read the extract below from Act 1, Scene 1 of *Romeo and Juliet* and identify the lines that demonstrate verbal conflict between the two households.

> **SAMPSON:** A dog of the house of Montague moves me.
>
> **GREGORY:** To move is to stir; and to be valiant is to stand: therefore, if thou art moved, thou runn'st away.
>
> **SAMPSON:** A dog of that house shall move me to stand: I will take the wall of any man or maid of Montague's.
>
> **GREGORY:** That shows thee a weak slave; for the weakest goes to the wall.
>
> **SAMPSON:** Tis true; and therefore women, being the weaker vessels, are ever thrust to the wall: therefore I will push Montague's men from the wall, and thrust his maids to the wall.
>
> **GREGORY:** The quarrel is between our masters and us their men.
>
> **SAMPSON:** 'Tis all one, I will show myself a tyrant: when I have fought with the men, I will be cruel with the maids, and cut off their heads.
>
> **GREGORY:** The heads of the maids?
>
> **SAMPSON:** Ay, the heads of the maids, or their maidenheads; take it in what sense thou wilt.
>
> **GREGORY:** They must take it in sense that feel it.
>
> **SAMPSON:** Me they shall feel while I am able to stand: and 'tis known I am a pretty piece of flesh.
>
> **GREGORY:** 'Tis well thou art not fish; if thou hadst, thou hadst been poor John. Draw thy tool! here comes two of the house of the Montagues.
>
> **SAMPSON:** My naked weapon is out. Quarrel, I will back thee.
>
> **GREGORY:** How? Turn thy back and run?
>
> **SAMPSON:** Fear me not.
>
> **GREGORY:** No, marry; I fear thee!

> **SAMPSON:** Let us take the law of our sides; let them begin.
>
> **GREGORY:** I will frown as I pass by, and let them take it as they list.
>
> **SAMPSON:** Nay, as they dare. I will bite my thumb at them;
>
> which is a disgrace to them, if they bear it.

3. At the end of this scene the Prince of Verona stops the fight and addresses the two heads of household. He threatens them with death should there be any more inter-family conflict in the streets of Verona. Now script the dialogue you would expect to occur between Lord Capulet and Lord Montague after the Prince's speech. Do you think they would apologise to each other; try to find a way to settle their disagreements; continue to be antagonistic?

Love–hate relationships

Introduction

In this lesson, students analyse the oxymorons used by Shakespeare in *Romeo and Juliet* to exemplify characters' mixed emotions. They debate the concept of love at first sight before looking at the scene in which Romeo and Juliet meet for the first time. Students create a monologue in role as the nurse, commenting on the unsuitable match.

Aims and objectives

- Analyse a range of texts or language uses, drawing on terminology related to literary, linguistic and grammatical features.
- Analyse and respond to the range of ideas and differing viewpoints, purposes and themes in a variety of related texts.

Starter (10 minutes)

Ask students to look at the range of quotations on the task sheet and spot the linguistic technique that is common to all of them. Explain that these extracts are taken from Romeo's speech about his unrequited love for Rosaline in Act 1 of *Romeo and Juliet*. Discuss how the use of contradictory language demonstrates the character's mixed emotions.

Main phase (40 minutes)

- Introduce the learning objectives and lesson outcomes: to explore the love–hate relationships that exist in the play and write a monologue in role as Juliet's nurse.
- Ask students whether they believe in love at first sight and discuss opinions. Read the extract from Act 1, Scene 5 in which Romeo and Juliet meet for the first time, and analyse the language used to show the strength of their emotions. Focus on the quotation 'My only love sprung from my only hate' and analyse.
- In role as Juliet's nurse, students write a monologue commenting on the unsuitable match and sharing their concerns about this potential relationship.

Plenary (10 minutes)

Students share best lines from their monologues and discuss how the audience would react to this scene; with fear, anticipation, joy?

Homework ideas

Ask students to create five new sentences including the oxymoron technique.

Make it easier!

Ask the students to create the monologues in groups so that they can share ideas.

Make it harder!

Compare this scene in two film versions of the play; Franco Zeffirelli and Baz Luhrmann (available on YouTube). Consider which director most successfully portrays the immense love that the characters experience when they fall in love and their anguish when they realise that they are from opposing families.

6:12 Love–hate relationships

1. Look at the quotations below. What do you notice about the language being used in each?

cold fire	heavy lightness

loving hate	sick health

2. Do you believe in love at first sight? Discuss your opinions with your partner.

The extracts below are taken from Act 1, Scene 5 of *Romeo and Juliet* in which the central characters first meet and fall in love. Read the text and identify any key quotes that show the extremity of their feelings.

> **ROMEO:** Then move not, while my prayer's effect I take.
>
> Thus from my lips, by yours, my sin is purged.
>
> **JULIET:** Then have my lips the sin that they have took.
>
> **ROMEO:** Sin from thy lips? O trespass sweetly urged!
>
> Give me my sin again.
>
> **JULIET:** You kiss by the book.
>
> **Nurse:** Madam, your mother craves a word with you.
>
> **ROMEO:** What is her mother?
>
> **Nurse:** Marry, bachelor,
>
> Her mother is the lady of the house,
>
> And a good lady, and a wise and virtuous
>
> I nursed her daughter, that you talk'd withal;
>
> I tell you, he that can lay hold of her
>
> Shall have the chinks.
>
> **ROMEO:** Is she a Capulet?
>
> O dear account! my life is my foe's debt.
>
> **BENVOLIO:** Away, begone; the sport is at the best.
>
> **ROMEO:** Ay, so I fear; the more is my unrest.
>
> **JULIET:** Come hither, nurse. What is yond gentleman?
>
> **Nurse:** The son and heir of old Tiberio.
>
> **JULIET:** What's he that now is going out of door?
>
> **Nurse:** Marry, that, I think, be young Petrucio.
>
> **JULIET:** What's he that follows there, that would not dance?
>
> **Nurse:** I know not.

JULIET: Go ask his name: if he be married.

My grave is like to be my wedding bed.

Nurse: His name is Romeo, and a Montague;

The only son of your great enemy.

JULIET: My only love sprung from my only hate!

Too early seen unknown, and known too late!

Prodigious birth of love it is to me,

That I must love a loathed enemy.

2. Imagine you are Juliet's nurse and you have just witnessed this scene and informed Juliet that the man that she has fallen for is a family enemy.

   Write a monologue in role as the nurse explaining how you feel about what has just occurred. Do you approve of this potential love match? What are you worried about?

© Helena Ceranic, 2011. *Resources for Teaching English: 11–14.*